Crimes, Confessions, *and* Convictions

Crimes, Confessions, *and* Convictions

Surviving Thirty Years in Law Enforcement

GARY DECKER

iUniverse, Inc.
Bloomington

Crimes, Confessions, and Convictions
Surviving Thirty Years in Law Enforcement

iUniverse books may be ordered through booksellers or by contacting:

iUniverse
1663 Liberty Drive
Bloomington, IN 47403
www.iuniverse.com
1-800-Authors (1-800-288-4677)

ISBN: 978-1-4759-8229-9 (sc)
ISBN: 978-1-4759-8230-5 (ebk)

Library of Congress Control Number: 2013905362

Printed in the United States of America

iUniverse rev. date: 03/25/2013

Contents

Introduction

In today's society, we are inundated with movies and TV programs covering big-city cops. When you turn on the TV, you can't help but see all the *CSI, Law and Order,* and *COPS* programs and watch the exciting lives of police officers from Miami, New York, Las Vegas, or Los Angeles. These officers are gifted in their abilities to collect massive amounts of evidence that will allow modern science, within the hour, to spit out the name of a suspect. The shows unfairly characterize all cops as quick to use force and not affected by traumatic events. You could also argue that such programs, along with true-crime novels, lead viewers and readers to believe that crime occurs only in large metropolitan areas and doesn't really affect rural places or small towns.

From my perspective of thirty years of police service, most of it spent in smaller Oregon communities, I can say that many citizens believe police officers are arrogant, badge-heavy ticket writers. Early on in my career, I realized that I was a little different than most officers. My friends were not just police officers. My wife and I had a good marriage, and we were active as a couple and then as a family with other couples and families mostly in my wife's circle. I found that our noncop friends were intrigued with my job but had no idea what kind of evil really exists. They told me I didn't fit the stereotype of a police officer. I'm not sure that I was different or if their perception came from a recent traffic ticket, which could have been their one and only encounter with a police officer. More recently, I have heard grumblings about the "luxurious" retirement packages for police officers and how, because of fiscal difficulties in the government, many are even calling for a change to these twenty-five-year pensions.

Everyone knows that police officers are different from other people. They go against the basic instinct to flee danger and are more than willing to go to it—into the school after the shooter, into a high speed pursuit to stop the armed robbers, or into countless buildings to search for the hidden felon. The US Department of Justice Bureau of Justice Statistics revealed that between 1976 and 1999, more than 1,800 law enforcement officers were killed in the line of duty.[1]

What media depictions of police and statistics don't show is the hidden killer of police officers. Police officers work in a high-stress environment and are, for the most part, sedentary. They work rotating shifts and are subject to being called in at any time. All of these factors have been studied and restudied, and the results are clear: police officers, specifically those from smaller agencies, with as little as nine years on the job face a significantly high mortality rates. Risks of cancer, cirrhosis of the liver, and heart disease are all substantially higher in police than what has been recorded in the average population. The studies go further to show that officers with thirty years on the job face more than three times the mortality rate of the general population.[2] [3]

Mentioned in the FBI Bulletin was the sad statistics relayed in a 2004 report by the National Police Suicide Foundation: in 2000, approximately four hundred police officers committed suicide.[4] This number was three times greater than the national average. According to Dr. Dan Goldfarb, in his speech written for Heavybadge.com, police officers also face a divorce rate between 60 and 75 percent,

---

[1] Brown, Jodi, and Langan, Patrick, Ph. D. "Policing and Homicide 1976-98" (March 2001): pg 21 US Department of Justice, Bureau of Justice Statistics, http://www.bjs.gov/content/pub/pdf/ph98.pdf

[2] Violanti, John M., "Dying from the Job: The Mortality Risk for Police Officers." Dr. Steve Davis Ministry and Leadership Resources. http://www.stevedavis.org/sol1art11.html.

[3] Lindsey, Dennis, and Kelly. Sean, "Issues in Small Town Policing." *FBI Law Enforcement Bulletin* 73, no. 7 (July 2004): 1-7. http://www.fbi.gov/stats-services/publications/law-enforcement-bulletin/2004-pdfs/july04leb.pdf.

[4] National Police Suicide Foundation, http://www.psf.org.

---

depending upon the study, while the national average remains at 50 percent.[5]

Researchers have also studied the life expectancy of police officers. The most commonly cited study was done by John M. Violanti, PhD, research associate professor in the University of Buffalo's Department of Social and Preventive Medicine. His forty-year study of police officers with between ten and nineteen years of service showed an average life expectancy of sixty-six years.[2] Other studies have shown life expectancy for police officers between fifty-three and sixty-six years of age.[6] At the same time, the average life expectancy in the United States is seventy-four years for men and eighty years for women.

What brought these risks home for me was the article "Issues in Small Town Policing" from the July 2004 *FBI Law Enforcement Bulletin*, as its authors suggested officers serving small towns were at even greater risk of these health issues partly because rural officers were not able to step away from the job.[3] No matter where the officers were at or what they were doing, people identified them as police officers, so they remained hyperaware and often, because they are identified as police officers and are expected to act, they are called into service while enjoying a family outing. Officers serving larger agencies have the luxury of anonymity while off duty and therefore can truly unwind and spend quality time with their families.

These numbers are just that—numbers—and I am sure everyone has heard the adage that statistics don't lie but liars use statistics. In 1998 my father, Roger Decker, retired at the age of sixty-two as Wallowa County Sheriff. He had spent over thirty years in police service, and prior to that, he spent twenty years in military service. In

---

[5] Goldfarb, Dan Ph.D. "The Effects of Stress on Police Officers", http://www.heavybadge.com/efstress.htm

[6] Aveni, Thomas, "Shift Work and Officer Survival" written for The Police Policy Studies Council, Issue #31, S & W Academy Newsletter (Summer 1999), http://www.theppsc.org/Staff_Views/Aveni/Shift-Survival.htm

---

October 1999, at the age of sixty-three, he died suddenly from a heart attack.

So to those who may question why police officers are allowed to retire early or to those whose only opinion of police comes from an undeserving traffic citation, I challenge you to look a little closer at what officers face and what sacrifices they make to provide us with a safer community.

Chapter One

Career Choices

I grew up in the 1960s and '70s; being a military brat, and later, at fourteen years old, I became the son of a police officer, I often wondered if I would end up in a career like my father's. I didn't give any occupation serious consideration because it seemed as though an eternity was ahead of me. I had a strong religious background and contemplated going into ministry, but after one year at Northwest College of the Assemblies of God, in Kirkland Washington, I realized I couldn't make the leap of faith necessary to become a minister. As a cop's kid, I didn't want my friends to think I was following in my father's footsteps, but no matter how many different careers I considered, the job of a police officer was the most intriguing, and it kept coming back to me as the only real choice.

I was the only son among four children. In our home, our father was the boss. He was the strong silent type. He never cried, at least not in front of us kids, and he almost never said "I love you." Public displays of affection, or PDA as it was known in the military, were forbidden and it appeared our dad was serious about not violating that military rule. My sisters and I knew where his attitude came from: our dad's mother from New Jersey. I really have to think hard to remember the times when I heard my grandmother say "I love you," and she too shied away from those awkward good-bye hugs.

Both Mom and Dad volunteered as EMTs, so this combined with Dad's police work made it natural that we had a police scanner on top of the refrigerator, always at such a volume that it could be heard throughout the house. Dad never talked about work, and only on a couple occasions did he mention threats to him or our family. It seemed to me that all cops were like Dad, never showing emotion and never talking about their concerns or the job.

I was a good student and enjoyed hunting, photography, and woodworking, but living in the small Northeast Oregon town of Wallowa, I still found times with nothing to do so I would make my way to our local police station and talk with the city's only other officer. He would tell me stories and show me some of their toys. During the CB radio era of the late '70s, I even agreed to use my '49 Chevy pickup as a stakeout vehicle in an effort to catch local thieves in action. Although I was never successful, the hunt and official use of my CB provided me with exhilaration that compared only to spotting the big buck on the season's opening morning.

I have fond memories of my father helping others. Once he came to the aid of our high school's second baseman. I was the team's centerfielder and watched my teammate as he dove for a ball and dislocated his shoulder then lay on the field in a great deal of pain. My dad, in uniform, came onto the field, hunched over the second baseman, and cradled his arms to relieve pressure and the accompanying pain. Dad stayed in this position until the ambulance arrived. The player later told me how much he appreciated what my dad did.

Now, I sit in my recliner and wonder where the last thirty-five years went. Last year I capped off thirty years of police work and was rewarded with the gift of "free time." This gift has given me an opportunity to view my cases as accomplishments and not as work.

I have always had a great deal of respect and appreciation for authority, and I think anyone that has known me, even before I had thoughts of going into the ministry, knew that I wanted to help others and to do what is right. I have come to learn that not only did these values mold me into the officer I was but were often the same values held by other police candidates. Unfortunately, what life's lessons have taught me is that no matter how strong my passion was, there was no way I could solve every case, help every victim, and hold every killer and rapist accountable. But I will always know that I gave it my all.

I look back at a seminar on child abuse and recall the instructor telling the story of a small boy walking along the beach where hundreds of starfish had washed ashore. As the boy walked along, he picked up starfish and put them back in the water. He did this again and again until a passerby, curious about the boy's activity, questioned him. The boy said he was saving the starfish. The curious man looked out at the hundreds of starfish still lying on the sand and told the young boy that there was no way he would ever save all of those starfish. The boy thought about this for a minute, and then he picked up another one and returned it to the water. He turned to the passerby and said, "I helped that one."

During my career, when I was knee-deep in a case, I never stopped to think of the magnitude of that case or think about what was next. I tried not to become overwhelmed by focusing on what I was presented with, dealing with it, and then moving on to the next case. Unfortunately, we live in a society where there is always a next case. When I was deciding on my career, I never dreamed that I would be involved in countless child molestation cases, several homicide cases, a couple of missing-persons cold cases, a serial rapist case, and two separate presidential-protection details or that I would finish my career by building the first ever sheriff's office livestock rescue.

Chapter Two

USAF Law Enforcement Specialist

In 1979, I had completed my first year at Northwest College and returned home to Wallowa to spend the summer. I started working at the local sawmill and realized that I could actually make money without a college education. I was able to pay off my first year of college and couldn't rationally leave the income to return to school, especially since I had no clear direction for my life.

That winter I went through several layoffs, and it was only then that I realized jobs in the lumber industry were not always reliable. In early 1980, I was waiting for my swing shift as I watched news of the hostages in Iran. I thought about my father's twenty-year air force career and how much I appreciated his commitment to our country. I guess it was only natural, with the heightened sense of patriotism during this time of crisis and with my new realism about the life, or lack of it, for someone in the lumber industry, that I started to give serious thought to joining the air force.

September 4, 1980, I lined up with other new recruits at the Boise Enlistment Center, and before long, I was on an airplane bound for Lackland Air Force Base in Texas. When I enlisted, I had been guaranteed a job as a law enforcement specialist. The air force had two separate security police fields: law enforcement, responsible for the main gate, basic base patrol, and dispatch duties for the entire base, and security specialists, primarily serving as guards of high-priority resources (planes, weapons, and facilities). While in basic training I was called out to take an aptitude test in both electronics and computers. I was told that everyone who scored 90 percent or higher on the basic military entrance exam, the ASVAB, was required to take additional aptitude tests. I took the tests and returned to my training unit. Later I was pulled out again, this time to talk with a career guidance counselor who told me that my aptitude test scores were high in both computers and electronics. He explained that ether of these jobs would be preferable to jobs in the security police, not to mention that they offered better training and reenlistment bonuses, which were not offered to law enforcement specialists. The counselor had the authority to change my field and get me started in a career that would more easily transfer to a civilian job. Me being the skeptic, I thought this was all a trick to get me to release my guaranteed law enforcement job so I could be placed in the career where the air force always needed more bodies, the security specialists. I imagined being assigned to a silo in North Dakota or a radar site in Alaska. No, I wouldn't fall for that, so I graciously turned the counselor down. That night I called home and talked with my father about the tests and the efforts to get me to change careers. It was then that I heard some concern in his voice about my choice to stay in law enforcement. I guess that because he was in law enforcement, he had a better understanding of the heartaches ahead and, as a father, he preferred his child to take the electronics or computer career.

I completed basic training and graduated as an honor graduate from the air force law enforcement academy. My first station was at RAF Greenham Common/RAF Welford in England. Who would have known that law enforcement specialists were still responsible for guarding nonnuclear weapons? *Guess dads may have some good insight after all.* I learned that not only did the law enforcement specialists guard weapons but, because of feuds between branches of service in Vietnam, the air force had also taken on the combat role of protecting any airfield under US control. So, I was given combat training and placed on a rapid deployment team. Members of our team got a series of vaccinations, and we were issued desert fatigues. I later learned that our team was under consideration for use in the Middle East, but that didn't happen. With the inauguration of Ronald Regan came the end of the Iran hostage crisis.

．　．　．

While stationed in England, the English government saw fit to start the buildup of Greenham Common for the ultimate deployment of cruise missiles. This brought in hundreds of protestors, mostly women, known as "Peace Campers." As their name implies, they set up camp outside the base and spoke out against the weapons buildup.

On January 1, 1982, my team was mobilized to the secured empty silos where Peace Campers had knocked down fences and entered the secure area. Our intelligence told us that they were armed with Molotov cocktails and crossbows. We had spent dozens of hours training on team riot formations and practicing lining up in formation and in unison everyone taking a step forward, stomping the front foot down then dragging the trailing foot forward, or as it was called the old stomp and drag, but all of this seemed to go out the window when our master sergeant ordered us to go after them, four of us to one of them, and watch each other's backs. I saw the fire department with their water cannon prepared and thought how unusual it was to see this on British soil, knowing that their citizens thought this type of force should be reserved for use in Ireland. We went in, and the protestors quickly surrendered. Protestors offered me "peace cookies," and I will never forget their repeating song lyrics of, "All we are saying is give peace a chance." I provided security at the back of an English bus and once we turned the buses over to the local authority we were done and returned to the base.

After leaving England, I learned that the Peace Campers were actually led by Russians and that they succeed in shutting down the base and keeping cruise missiles out of England.

．　．　．

I also recall, with some humor, our constant training. It seemed that we were always preparing for invasions or break-ins. During one training session, I was asked to take on the role of an intruder at one of the installation's high-risk facilities. I made my way to the dark side of the building and positioned myself flat on my back, beret covering my face, both feet planted against a large pipe that came from the building and went into the ground. I lay there for about five minutes and listened to the security team approach. I saw shadows of two officers as they approached my position, tactically keeping their flashlights off, knowing if they used them it would give their position away. The officer closest to the building stepped over the pipe and continued on. The second, walking behind the other and further from the building, was heading right at me. I tried not to panic, knowing full well this was only an exercise, and chose to do nothing. Then I felt the officer's foot on my thighs as he started to step right on me. To my surprise, he lifted his foot and stepped over me. *How nice of him,* I thought, as he and his partner completed the search and gave the all clear. The team of five then gathered in the light from the front of the building approximately fifteen feet from my location. I stood up, walked to the corner, and said, "You're all dead," surprising them. The sergeant was not happy, and this only meant more exercises. During the next one, I was captured, and I could tell my teammates were not happy with me, as they showed no mercy in shoving me to the ground and cuffing me.

.   .   .

Men on our team worked three swing shifts, three graveyard shifts, and then had three days off. The graveyard shift was extremely boring, and we were always looking for ways to stay busy to make the shift bearable. I took an interest in the nocturnal rabbits and hedgehogs. One night I actually caught a small rabbit and put it into the back of my Sherpa (a patrol pickup). By coincidence, just afterward, a base exercise was called, and I was assigned to listening post-observation post 2. I parked my Sherpa on the west side of LPOP 2 and made my way to a position where I had a clear view to the east and north, thinking the assault would come from one of these directions. About fifteen minutes into our exercise, I heard someone shouting out "Bang Bang Bang!". Then I heard the assailant yell, "I got you!" I turned around and saw the intruder in the open approaching my Sherpa. He yelled, "I heard you! You're dead!" From my position above him and approximately fifty yards away, I shouted back, "Bang! You're dead." He was convinced that the noise coming from my Sherpa was me and was pissed that a rabbit had caused him to give his position away and conclude our exercise.

.   .   .

Military life was not always easy for me. I was not used to being around those who lived by different values and standards from mine. After being in England for about a year, my team received a new flight chief, a senior master sergeant who had chosen to move to England and leave his wife and kids back in the States so his tour would be shortened to only two years. However, he had chosen to move his girlfriend over to live with him. His work-related decisions showed the same lack of judgment, and this concerned me.

Our country was not at war, but we needed to be prepared for all situations, and we did this through training and following copious rules and regulations. The US government even put these in a book, the *Uniform Code of Military Justice* (UCMJ), which contained rules prohibiting adultery, oral sex, and flipping the bird (giving "provoking speeches or gestures"). As anyone who has been in the military will tell you, very little effort was put into holding everyone accountable for all violations.

One specific operating procedure was, upon arriving for duty, to inspect your post and only accept it from the off-going guard after it passed inspection. On our swing shifts, replacement guards were often assigned while the guard for the day ate dinner. One day I was assigned as the relief, and since we were in England, it was no surprise that we had rain and plenty of it. The off-going guard was extremely busy with pass collection and constantly going in and out of the post. Understanding that we had no time for pleasantries, I quickly accepted the post and immediately immersed myself in the pass-collection process. The activity subsided, and about forty-five minutes after I took the post, the duty guard arrived and relieved me.

Two hours into the shift, the senior master sergeant decided to conduct an inspection of the post, and he found dirt on the floor. The guard, a buck sergeant, blamed me for it. I was called to the entry post, and the senior master sergeant belittled me in front of others, saying I had accepted a dirty post. I tried to explain that this was the only way during the rush hour that we could transfer responsibilities. I also pointed out the obvious, that the buck sergeant had accepted the still-dirty post from me. The senior master sergeant saw little merit in my argument and assigned me to mop the floor. When I had finished, being a little disappointed in my boss, I asked that he return to inspect the floor. He did, and while I stood at attention, I suggested that I be allowed to wax the floor. The senior master sergeant didn't think my request was as humorous as I did, but he took me up on my suggestion. At the completion of this task, I again called him to the post. Once again standing at attention, I explained that while waxing the floor I had looked out and had seen that the Sherpa could use a good cleaning. He had then had enough and ordered me into his office. He made it clear that he did not appreciate my behavior and that he would be watching me.

I had a hunch that he had spoken to some of the buck sergeants and that I was now a target. A few weeks later, at the completion of our swing shift, another airman and I were talking as we entered the clearing-barrel area. I don't recall specifically what we were saying, but it had nothing to do with safety and clearing procedures, which was a violation of standard operation procedures. While I was standing outside the clearing area, I said something to the airman, who was inside the area, and he started laughing. The buck sergeant inside the area then told the airman to proceed, at which time the airman emptied his weapon and the sergeant then visually inspected it before being allowed to depart. The airman and I completed the process without further comment from the buck sergeant or another buck sergeant standing right outside the area. Once we had turned in our weapons and were heading to the bus, I saw the two sergeants talking and then watched them as they head toward the senior master sergeant's office. Within a few minutes, the other airman and I were pulled from the bus by a buck sergeant and ordered to the senior master sergeant's office. We stood at attention in front of the senior master sergeant's desk, and the two buck sergeants stood off to the side.

The senior master sergeant told us that we had violated SOPs for clearing-barrel safety and that disciplinary action would be taken against us. I agreed with the senior master sergeant that we had been talking and that our conversation had nothing to do with safety procedures, but I also explained that this happens dozens of times each day. I further explained that the SOPs not only say that each participant is required to abide by the procedures but also that the clearing-barrel supervisor, or any observing NCO for that matter, who witnesses a violation is to immediately stop all activity and correct the behavior before allowing the clearing process to continue. I said I understood that we were in violation and were going to be disciplined, but I also believed that the buck sergeants should be held to the same standard. The senior master sergeant then instructed me and the other airman to leave his office. As we stepped out into the hall, the airman praised me for my response and said he felt there was no way they would take any action against us, and he was right. A few minutes, later we were called back in and given a warning.

. . .

One fond memory from my European tour happened in Polebrook, England. I was part of an honor guard dedicating a memorial to all of Polebrook's servicemen who served in Operation Market Garden. Being able to talk with a few men who were part of one of the largest military operations in world history and to hear their stories was fascinating. I later researched Operation Market Garden and found that the number of casualties was between fifteen thousand and seventeen thousand. How small this memorial now seemed for so many lives.

. . .

After spending two years in England I completed my four years of service as a security police desk sergeant at Mather AFB in Sacramento, California. I was stationed there shortly after a B-52 had crashed on takeoff. I heard that the crash was caused by pilot error. I understand that he had used a "wet thrust," which was too hot and fast for a multiple-plane takeoff. He then made the error of powering back on the throttle, which caused an engine shut-down. Because of his lack of elevation, he didn't have the time to power back up, and he crashed. Shortly after I arrived another incident happened to a B-52. During the refueling, there was a failure, by an airman, to remove or open a vent plug. Therefore, when the fuel was pumped into a wing under pressure, the wing broke, and we had a major jet-fuel spill.

We desk sergeants were always evaluated and observed, and of course, since this base had recently experienced negative events, we constantly performed exercises. During one of these, I was given the location of a possible explosive device. I quickly plotted it on the map, and using the cordon grids, positioned control points at each entrance into the area. Shortly after giving my directions, a master sergeant radioed from the field and instructed me to move some of my posts. I adjusted my map and confirmed each of the assignments as he wanted them. Next came radio traffic from the captain, who, having now had the chance to view the assignments on his own map, chose to move them once again, closer to their original positions. I dutifully plotted the new map and confirmed his requested assignments. While this was going on, I could not help but see the evaluator busily writing. Shortly after the exercise, I was told that the evaluator had highly praised my actions but gave our sergeants and officers low marks.

. . .

While at Mather, I did what everyone always said not to do: volunteer. Law enforcement officers from every branch of the service were requested to serve a ninety-day temporary duty assignment (TDA) at Fort Lewis, Washington. The government saw the need to expand the jail there into something of a mini-Fort Leavenworth to take on prisoners from all branches of the service. With plans for an immediate build-up, they needed officers to work as guards until permanent guards could be assigned.

I was one of four air force senior airmen assigned to the position of desk-clerk. The job had a steep learning curve, which involved not only getting used to the duties but also acclimating to the culture of other branches of the service. The desk clerks were the only ones assigned to a rotating shift: we worked three day shifts, three swing shifts, three graveyard shifts, and then had three days off. This schedule provided me with a clear understanding of the reasoning behind never volunteering. Prior to my return to Mather, an army staff sergeant told me how impressed he was with all of the airmen. I asked why we, the senior airmen, had been chosen to handle the more difficult jobs given that we would only be there for a short time, and the staff sergeant responded, "You air force guys can type." He ended by saying he would put me in for a medal, but I guess it got lost in the mail.

.   .   .

It was now October 1983, and I was back at Mather AFB, where our rapid deployment team was placed on alert. We gathered at the large airport hangar and got busy accounting for all of our gear. We weren't sure exactly what was going on, but our commander assured us it was not a drill. We spent most of the day at the hangar, and then early that evening, we were released. Rumors spread quickly, and shortly, those rumors were confirmed: US forces had been deployed to Granada, and our rapid deployment team was considered for inclusion. However, the team from down the road at Travis AFB was deployed instead.

Toward the end of my enlistment, I met with the colonel, and he pitched reenlistment to me. He promised me my choice of duty selection and, inevitably, promotion to staff sergeant. When I told him I had decided to return to civilian life and to pursue a career in law enforcement, he changed tack and told me that I was dreaming if I thought getting a police job would be easy.

Three months after separating from the air force, I had my first job offer, from Boardman Department of Public Safety.

Chapter Three

Boardman Department of Public Safety

Boardman, a small community with a port on the Columbia River that has always been known for its french fries, had a large Hispanic population. Interstate 84 ran through it, and traffic flowed into the community regardless of the time of day, so if nothing else, a young police officer could always look for minor traffic violations to stay busy. Although Boardman was a small town, with less than two-thousand residents, it still had four drinking establishments, and I found myself responding to them repeatedly. The Department of Public Safety employed a chief, a sergeant, and two officers. The chief was also responsible for the fire department, and I was cross-trained as a fireman. The chief and sergeant worked days, so I and the other officer worked four twelve-hour shifts and had four days off.

Day one was February 1, 1985. I rode with a veteran officer who was in his early fifties and had been a sergeant with another agency before that agency downsized. It had snowed, and most of the roads were still covered in ice. Our first radio call was an attempt to locate (ATL) for a stolen vehicle along with the owners purse that came from nearby Umatilla County.

It couldn't have been more than thirty minutes before we rounded a corner and came upon a car stuck in the snow accompanied by its driver. The driver had left the car in Drive and was standing behind it, trying to push it through the slick patch. The veteran officer told me to cover him, and he casually walked up behind the man and asked if he needed some help. The officer got close, as though he was going to help push the car, and simply grabbed the man's arms and placed him in handcuffs. This turned out to be the stolen car, and inside it was the purse. I thought this job was going to be easy.

This officer didn't last too long with the agency. I later talked with the chief about some of his behavior, including what once happened while he trained me. Early in our graveyard shift, we observed a car drive past a freeway off-ramp stop sign, back up, and then drive into a nearby parking lot. This seemed to me to be an ordinary traffic stop for disobeying a stop sign. We both got out of the vehicle, and the officer talked with the driver, an attractive woman traveling alone. She said she was tired and was pulling off the road to get some rest. The veteran officer gave her a warning, which seemed appropriate, and we both returned to the patrol car, only to have him tell me to stay in the car while he reengaged the woman. Immediately after this stop the officer told me my shift was over, and he took me home. The next day, he told me that he had taken the woman to his apartment, and although he didn't give much detail, he said she was great in bed. The chief apologized to me for having to see that side of our job and hoped I didn't believe everyone was like this.

.   .   .

After completing training at the Oregon Police Academy, I returned to Boardman, where I was recognized as a finalist for a prestigious award covering all areas of study, including academics, fitness, and firearms. During one of my first solo shifts, I went to the freeway overpass to respond to a cow-at-large call. I didn't know much about cattle, but I soon learned that if they didn't want to move, there wasn't much I could do to encourage them. A passerby stopped and showed me the trick of twisting the cow's tail to encourage it to move, and although it worked, I hoped I would not need to use that trick again. Not only the chief but the local paper found this call interesting, and after the story was published, everyone in the community knew me as the award finalist who could handle loose cattle.

I didn't waste much time in purchasing my own police scanner, and just as my dad had done, I placed it on top of the refrigerator and turned it up so that no matter the time of day or night, I could hear what was happening.

.   .   .

With Boardman being located along the Columbia River came beach parties. I once pulled over a suspected drunk driver and found an attractive young lady behind the wheel wearing only a bikini. I had a deputy stop by to assist, but he was called away to handle a domestic-disturbance call in my jurisdiction. I was stuck processing this young lady while the deputy, I later learned, had to arrest a drunk, overweight, abusive husband wearing only his underwear. Not something the deputy would soon forget or let me forget.

.   .   .

Once, as I sat along I-84, I watched a car slow down in the westbound lane, make a U turn, and head east, still in the westbound lanes. I called the vehicle description in to dispatch, and I pursued from the eastbound lanes. I activated my lights and siren and I used my spotlight to get the driver to pull over. The pursuit continued for about five minutes, and I feared there would be a head-on collision. Unsure where the closest backup was, I decided to act. I went against training and crossed over to the westbound lanes to pursue the suspect from behind. It seemed to work, and I pulled over behind the vehicle. Once stopped, I noticed that a deputy had also arrived from the opposite direction. As I approached the suspect, thinking that he would only be intoxicated, the deputy said, "Watch out, Decker. I saw him reach under the seat." I stepped back to the safety of my patrol car and ordered the driver out of his car. He complied, and in his hand was a set of homemade nunchakus. I greatly appreciated the presence of the deputy, and he and I gained a great deal of respect for each other. This same deputy set me up on a blind date and then stood as my best man when I married this same woman, whom I have now been married to for over twenty-five years.

. . .

A few other events stand out from my experience in Boardman. Once, before I fully knew all of the streets and subdivisions, dispatch received a call that a small child had been found floating in a swimming pool. This was before 911 provided addresses automatically, and the caller was having trouble giving her address, so the dispatcher was not very helpful relaying the information to me. That feeling in the pit of my stomach was awful. Here was a child that needed help, and we were unable to clearly understand where the child was. Once I had an idea of the residential area, I told the dispatcher to have the mother take the child out to the road so I would see her. This worked. I found the woman running toward me holding the lifeless child. I had been certified as an EMT, so I had mentally prepared to provide CPR on the way, but as soon as the mother handed the child to me, the child threw up all over me. I guess the jarring from the mother's run was as good as chest compressions.

A few weeks later a motorist coming off of I-84 flagged me down and said there was a bad accident two miles west. I radioed it in and immediately responded. As I pulled up, I saw a van overturned onto its top. Several other vehicles were also stopped. As I approached the van, I found a baby still wrapped in a blanket lying about fifty feet in front of it. I checked for a pulse and found none; a small amount of fluid was coming from the child's ear, and the child's eyes were already glazed over. I covered its head with the blanket and started to move closer to the van when a truck driver insisted that I couldn't give up on the child and had to do more. I told him that I didn't need him to criticize me, and if he didn't want to be constructive, then he could just leave. I then came face-to-face with the mother, looking for her child. She had head injuries and told me that the child had been asleep on her lap when the van rolled. She further explained that her family, of six along with the children's grandmother, was returning from a family picnic. I told her that someone was with her child and that she needed to stay with the rest of her family, who were now huddled around the other side of the van.

I asked the truck driver to gather blankets from passer-bys and to stay with the family while I went to check on the grandmother. I saw her head and hands pinned between the van's sliding door and the ground. I wanted to get inside to see if I could do anything for her. The glass had been broken out of the windshield, so I crawled through. I got a few cuts on my hands, but nothing to be concerned with. From the initial inspection and seeing the unnatural position of her legs I realized that the grandmother had numerous broken bones and that I would not be able to help from inside the van, so I crawled back out and used my hands to dig out the dirt from around her head and hands. Not knowing if she was dead, I talked to her as I dug. She then grabbed my hand and squeezed it. I heard sirens and knew that I had some help, so I felt comfortable staying in place with this grandmother. Then the ambulance attendant arrived, casually opened the van's back doors, and walked in. I made a mental note that I should always try the obvious before making my job more difficult.

Air Life was called in to transport the grandmother to a hospital, but she ultimately died from her injuries. While still on the accident scene, the medical examiner approached me and asked about the child. I walked with him to the child and watched as he removed the blanket, only to see the child's face covered in ants. I felt helpless and inadequate. This loss was something I never expected. For the next few weeks, I struggled to sleep and kept being awakened by images of the child and words from the truck driver saying I had to do more.

It may have been a coincidence, or maybe the medical examiner saw the hurt in my eyes that night of the accident, whatever the reason, a few weeks later he stopped by the diner while I was on a coffee break and casually asked how I was doing. I explained that the child's death bothered me, but I knew I wasn't the first to go through something like this, so I was confident that I would be okay. He said that he had heard about the child in the swimming pool and how, because of my actions, that child was alive. He explained that bad things were always going to happen and all that anyone could ask for was that someone like me would be there for them when they needed help. He said there was nothing medical I could have done that would have helped the child in the accident, and he, for one, was glad I had chosen to be there for that family and this community.

. . .

My time in Boardman wasn't all work. I continued my college education and learned to golf. My deputy friend and I would golf during our days off, and on one of these days, we were crossing the freeway overpass when we saw two uniformed corrections officers talking with two men. The men shoved the corrections officers and ran toward the wildlife refuge, which was next to the freeway. We stopped and identified ourselves, and the guards explained that the men had escaped. We drove to the end of the frontage road and jumped out, without guns, handcuffs, or radios. About a half mile into the refuge, we caught up with the first man. He had stopped and tried to hide in the grass. The deputy and I took him down at fingerpoint, and I used an arm bar to lock his arm between my chest and his back and controlled him by his shoulder with my other arm. I left the deputy behind and walked the man out to the nearest house and yelled for the homeowners. They came out, and at my direction, they called in to dispatch. A state police car arrived fairly quickly.

When I got to the PD, the sergeant was busy on the radio and on the phone coordinating the many different resources that had responded to the call of the escape. About fifteen minutes later, the deputy arrived just the same way I had. He also had walked out of the refuge with his prisoner and gotten a neighbor to call in for the uniformed ride. It was then that we learned that the corrections van was an Immigration and Naturalization Services (INS) van and the two who had escaped were just suspected of being illegal immigrants. Neither the deputy nor I thought much about this; we both believed we were doing just what any other officer would do. The following week, the local paper ran a story recognizing the sergeant for his quick action in calling for assistance, resulting in both escapees being captured in less than thirty minutes. I found this humorous, but the deputy thought it was just wrong for the sergeant not to have spoken up and given credit where it was due.

· · ·

I once responded to an alarm at a tavern. In checking the perimeter, I found the doorjamb of the back door broken and a visible shoe print in the center of the door. Impatient, I decided not to wait for my backup and went in. While making my way through the building, I peeked around a corner and saw someone moving around. I lit him up with my flashlight, identified myself, and asked him who he was and what he was doing. He was about seventeen-years-old, standing about three inches taller and weighing about twenty-five pounds more than me. He said he lived next door and had seen someone break in and followed them. At about this time both my sergeant and a barmaid arrived. The sergeant stayed with the teen while I completed the check of the building. No one else was inside. I talked with the youth and poked holes in his story, while the sergeant appeared to be flirting with the barmaid. After checking the kid's shoes, I knew I had the one responsible for the break-in. I told him he was under arrest and to put his hands behind his back. He refused and, raising his voice, said I was not going to cuff him behind his back. The sergeant seemed a bit distracted by the shouting, and in an effort to get back to his conversation, he told me that he knew the kid and his father so it would be fine to cuff his hands in front.

I took the teen home. I told him I wanted to tell his father what had happened and get him another pair of shoes before we went to the juvenile department. We went to the back door of a single-wide manufactured home. I knocked and identified myself, and a male voice told me to come in. I stood in the hallway, adjacent the father's bedroom, a bathroom, and the teen's bedroom. I told the father what had happened and explained that his son was being arrested for burglary. The father, who I can only assume was intoxicated, never got out of bed. The boy, who still had his hands cuffed in front of him, and I went to the boy's bedroom, and he grabbed a pair of football cleats. He started to put them on when I told him that I was also going to confiscate the marijuana and bong that were in plain view. He told me he watched all of the police shows and knew that I couldn't do that without a search warrant. I calmly told him that he was wrong and that I was going to seize them. He stood up and came right at me, saying, "I'm going to kill you." I took a step back, put my hand out, and told him to stop. I was in the hallway again when he lunged at me and grabbed hold of my revolver, which stayed in its holster. I locked his hands down with my right hand, and with my left hand on the back of his shoulder, I turned him toward the exterior door and pushed. I heard the glass on the door break but was only focused on his grip of my gun, which had not changed with the breaking glass. In fact, he was able to pull my entire belt around. I knew I had to step in front of him and try to get him to the ground. Keeping pressure on his hands, I again pivoted him around, this time forcing him face-first into the bathroom door. His grip on my gun had now weakened and he grabbed the doorknob. The father yelled, "You two knock it off!" like we were a couple of kids wrestling around. During the entire incident the father still did not feel the need to get out of bed. I was now able to control the teen's left wrist, and I pushed him toward the sink. The bathroom door then broke from its hinges, and I found myself on top of him, pushing his hands up behind his back and at the same time pushing his face down into the sink. I'm not sure how long it was before I realized I had control and he was now crying. I used the youth's brief surrender to adjust the handcuffs behind his back and take him out to the patrol car.

I hated to do it, but I thought I should interrupt the sergeant's social hour and get him to my location. He responded and was apologetic about the advice to cuff in front, and he gladly stood by as I gathered the marijuana, bong, and shoes. This was the first time that I had my life threatened, and although my firearm never left my holster, I had several weeks of poor sleep afterward. Each time I got to sleep, I would relive this incident, hearing the shouts that he was going to kill me, and wake in a cold sweat. In my nightmare, the suspect removed my handgun and each scenario ended with it being used, either against me or him. I became extremely cautious going through that neighborhood, always thinking the teen may have a rifle and want to finish what he started.

. . .

The same bar was later the scene of a bar fight between whites and Hispanics. The chief had said that because we were without backup, we should never arrive unannounced. Well ahead of my arrival, I had activated my lights and siren and made sure not to speed or violate any other traffic laws. When I entered, I encountered lots of shouting and chaos. In an effort to separate the parties, I asked all of the Hispanics to wait outside for me. Then, when I failed to get one person to talk at a time—too much for the intoxicated to comprehend—I asked the barmaid to explain what happened. She said that one of the Hispanics had started the fight, adding that she would point him out. We both stepped outside only to find that all of the Hispanics had left. She then openly criticized my actions, and I explained that we were living in a community where I was the only officer on duty. I told her I would be open to hearing how she thought a lone officer could control a fight involving twenty people. She said nothing else.

. . .

While patrolling during a graveyard shift, an approaching car failed to dim its high-beam headlights. This was on surface streets near a residential area, so I assumed it was a drunk heading home. I radioed in the license number and made the stop. There were no streetlights, but with my spotlight, I could see the driver's seat fairly easily. As I approached, I heard dispatch call out to my nearest cover officer and say that I had just gone out on a stolen-vehicle. I was about even with the other car's back door and started to panic. I asked to see the driver's hands and did a quick check of the seat. I saw a ski mask and paper sack on the seat next to him. Unsure of exactly what to do, I stepped back toward the trunk of his car and ordered him to step out. He immediately ducked toward the paper sack. I retreated behind the driver's door of my patrol car and informed dispatch that I had a subject not complying with my commands.

I gave the driver several more commands, which went unanswered, and feeling like I was in a poor position if he were to bail out on the passenger's side, I moved around to the right side of my trunk. I waited for several minutes, and finally a deputy arrived. He barked out orders, and finally the subject exited the car to be taken into custody. The adrenalin rush was unique, and I found that at the end of the shift, it was extremely hard to unwind and get to sleep.

. . .

After working in Boardman for about a year and a half, the chief approached me and asked what I thought about La Grande Police Department. I told him that I had previously applied with them but was told that they wanted to hire a certified officer. The chief went on to say that the lieutenant had called and told him that La Grande was interested in hiring me, but knowing that I hadn't been with Boardman for very long, the lieutenant hadn't wanted to approach me with an offer without first getting the chief's approval. I told the chief that I believed I owed him at least two years, but he said that he didn't want to keep anyone from his career goals but also that he had been fighting with the city council to raise officers' pay to an amount that would encourage quality candidates to remain with the agency. He said he had been losing that battle, and if I chose to leave for La Grande, he could use my departure as a means to institute more suitable pay for the next officer. With his blessing, I applied for and was hired at La Grande Police Department.

Chapter Four

La Grande Police Department

La Grande was a small college town with a population of about ten thousand nestled in the mountains of Northeast Oregon in Union County, neighbor to where my father was sheriff, Wallowa County. When I was in high school, La Grande was mentioned on Paul Harvey's radio show as a community where you would most likely be able to get away with murder. This reputation came from two unsolved homicide cases, one of a barmaid who was brutally attacked with a hatchet and left to die in Candy Cane Park, the second of a woman walking on Morgan Lake Road, a steep gravel road about one mile long from La Grande to a small lake. The Candy Cane Park murder did ultimately result in a conviction, but it was later overturned on a technicality. The Morgan Lake murder was never solved.

I started my new job in July of 1986. La Grande Police Department worked in three shifts: days, 6:00 a.m. to 2:00 p.m.; swing, 2:00 p.m. to 10:00 p.m.; and graveyard, 10:00 p.m. to 6:00 a.m. Officers would rotate shifts each quarter, with every officer required to work at least one of each of the shifts over the year with the choice of the fourth shift determined by seniority. I was hired at the same time as second officer and already felt good about having immediate backup. Our training period was pretty informal, and in August, just after being released on my own, I was called in to work scene security at a homicide.

An unidentified woman lay on a bed inside the apartment. She was covered by a sleeping bag. Once we removed the bag, we found she was naked with her face and head covered in dried blood. The odor indicated she had been there for a few days. I followed basic instructions to allow only the investigators in unless the detective gave his approval and to be sure to document when anyone went in and when they came out. Seemed pretty simple until a man arrived and asked what was happening. I explained we were in the middle of an investigation, and he said he knew the male resident and asked if the resident was okay. I was in the process of writing the resident's name in my notebook when the man asked if this had anything to do with Cindy. "Who?" I asked, and he said, "Cindy O'Neil." He pointed to a bike leaning on a rail at the end of the hallway and explained that Cindy owned it. I called the detective, and he and the man were soon off to the police department for a more in-depth interview.

That night, the crime lab arrived at the scene, and these investigators asked if I wanted to step in to see what they do. That was an invitation I could not pass up. They waited until dark to mix their luminol, and then they sprayed it around the bed and on the walls and floor in the rest of the apartment. Each of the specks of blood glowed green when exposed to this mixture, making it easy to see blood-splash patterns. The technicians identified three clear cast-offs of blood, signaling that there were at least four blows to the face, the first causing the blood to flow and each subsequent blow resulting in a cast-off when the weapon was raised.

Near the body were duct tape, a bottle of oil, and a chair, with a hard, smooth plastic seat cover, that sat next to the bed. In the chair I could see the outline of male buttocks and testicles. The technician also pointed to fluid that appeared to come from the chair toward the bed. He suggested that the suspect had masturbated in the chair and believed that tests of the samples he collected would confirm this. We could see footprints across the floor and a glow around the sink, where it appeared the assailant had cleaned up.

The following day, the other new officer and I were asked if we wanted to attend the autopsy. We responded with a resounding yes.

Once we entered the room, the experienced detective offered me cotton swabs with a few drops of wintergreen oil on them. I declined. Although I positioned myself about three feet from the body, once the doctor performed the Y cut, I couldn't help myself. The other officer and I, in unison, stepped back to the wall. I wished I had accepted the scented cotton balls. The doctor's opinion was that the victim actually died from suffocation while lying facedown on the blood-soaked pillow.

The investigation focused on the tenant of the room where our victim was located. All of the interviews indicated that the tenant was the last person to be seen with Cindy and he had not been seen in La Grande since. The detective made a trip to California, the suspect's former home, and immediately upon contacting the suspect, the man said that he figured the detective was there to talk about the girl in his room. He confessed, saying that he and the victim had been partying and returned to his room for sex. She resisted the idea of anal intercourse, and he then beat and bound her and carried out his will, even after thinking she may have been dead, using oil to facilitate the sexual act.

This investigation, although the crime was gruesome, left me wanting to become a detective. It had the opposite effect on the other new hire. He resigned within a couple of weeks, saying he didn't think he was cut out for this job.

.   .   .

On June 13, 1987, the body of a woman was found along I-84 just east of La Grande. The remains were later identified as Lisa Szubert, who had last been seen in Mountain Home, Idaho, with a man at a truck stop. Witnesses provided a description of the man, including that "JUNE" was tattooed on his knuckles. This description led to Darren Dee O'Neall, and it wasn't long before he was on the FBI's most-wanted list and then behind bars. Darren O'Neall ultimately pleaded guilty to murder in Washington and received a life sentence for taking the lives of at least six women, Lisa Szubert being his last victim. I remembered thinking how evil exists everywhere.

Even though we thought we were isolated in this small community of Eastern Oregon, we were not exempt.

. . .

Day shifts on Sundays were generally our quietest. This Sunday morning's solitude was interrupted by a radio call reporting a man, wearing only his underwear, busting into a residence and screaming something about murder and shouting that "they" were after him. I was close by the residence, and I found the family waiting in the street. They said they had no idea who the crazed intruder was and that he was still inside their home.

I started toward the house when the man—midtwenties, approximately five feet nine inches and one hundred sixty-five pounds—came to the front door. I asked him to come on outside, which he did, and I asked him what was going on. He jerked his head around and showed no indication that he could remain focused on any one subject. He repeated that "they" were after him and continued to make quick head and eye movements, shifting his focus from my baton on my left hip to my weapon on my right and back. He circled to my left, and I ordered him to sit down on the ground. He ignored my order and moved closer to me, continuing to shift his focus from my baton to my weapon. I told him I would place him in handcuffs for the safety of both of us if he didn't sit down. He then lunged toward my baton. I grabbed his left arm and pivoted away from him, pushing his shoulder to the ground. Once on the ground, I tried to pull his left arm behind his back, but he made a quick rolling motion, as if he were trying swing around behind me. I dropped all of my weight onto the middle of his back to stop his roll, but I was then struggling to pull his hands out from under his body. I ordered him again to put his hands behind his back and to stop resisting. We struggled for what seemed like an eternity, but was probably no more than two minutes, until my backup arrived. Once he had the weight of two of us on his back and one on each arm, we were able to cuff him. I then gave him an ultimatum: get up and walk to the car or be dragged there like an animal. He said he was done resisting and would walk. He did, and I was able to take a breath once I had shut him into the back of the caged patrol car.

I had once heard a comedian joke about witnesses being excited after seeing a shocking event, and I think this woman's response would have worked well into the routine. The first thing she said to me was, "Oh my god, did you see that?" She recovered nicely by asking if I was okay, but I did find some humor in her statement.

It was not a surprise to learn that the suspect had been using meth the night before. The cuffs seemed to bring him down, and he began talking like we were friends. I told him that he was a handful and could have gotten himself hurt. He responded by saying he had been a state-champion wrestler and didn't expect me to be able to keep him down.

.   .   .

I was with another officer when we received information of a suspected drug deal that had just occurred. The caller gave a specific license plate number and description of a driver and vehicle. The caller also reported witnessing the driver place scales and packages into the trunk of the car. The other officer and I set up to intercept the car, and sure enough, along it came. The driver was speeding, so we now had probable cause for the stop. He was cooperative during the stop, and we asked him if he had any drugs or drug paraphernalia in the car. He said he did not. We then asked him if he would allow us to search his car, and he agreed. He opened the trunk for us, where we found the scales the witness mentioned and packages of meth. We arrested the man, and the case was soon before the court in a motion to suppress evidence. The judge ruled in favor of the suspect, stating that because we had not turned off our overhead lights, the driver wouldn't have believed he was free to go and therefore could not have voluntarily consented to the search.

The case was thrown out, and although I disagreed with that, I could adapt to the changing rules. This wasn't the end of the case. The suspect elected to sue the department and me personally. During his deposition, he lied and said that he gave his consent only because I had pointed my service weapon at him and he felt threatened. I felt completely abandoned when I learned that the city's attorneys had settled the civil suit by paying the plaintiff off, explaining that the decision was not based on what was right or wrong but rather on what was least expensive for the agency.

While trying to cope with a sense of abandonment, I questioned why I was so willing to donate time to the city. My wife and I discussed my need to do a better job of separating my home life from my work life. On that very day, we went for a walk around the college campus, and as we passed the tennis courts, a fight broke out. I immediately stepped in, identifying myself as an off-duty officer and breaking up the fight. My wife was quick to point out that my commitment to keep from bringing my job home lasted for less than thirty minutes.

I did start doing more woodworking and got back into photography to help keep my mind off work. I also removed the police scanner from my home. Shortly afterward, we went out to enjoy a pizza. As we walked into the restaurant, I saw the driver, who had been paid off for lying about me, working as a waiter. Now we had to question when and where we would go out to eat.

.   .   .

It was midafternoon when dispatch advised that a caller shopping in Safeway had recognized a wanted felon. My partner and I responded. We planned to park on the side of the store out of view from the exit and wait for the subject to leave. The one thing we didn't count on was shoppers fascinated by our presence talking about the police when they entered the store. Just as our subject exited the store, he noticed people stopping and looking around the corner, and he quickly retreated back into the store.

The jig was up, so I followed him into the store. I shouted, "Police! Freeze!" He stopped, started to raise his hands and turn away, and suddenly the chase was on. We went up and down the aisles like we were running an obstacle course, avoiding people, carts, and displays. We turned toward the stock room and my radio fell out of its quick-release holster. It cluttered and skidded across the floor just as the suspect tried leaping a flat stocking cart. He lost his balance and fell into a bread rack. I was right on his heels, and before he knew it, I had my cuffs on him.

Later that evening I called home, and my wife asked if I was okay. I said I was, and she told me that someone she knew had been in Safeway and had seen the chase. The person said, "It was just like *T.J. Hooker.* Your husband was chasing the guy and threw his radio at the guy's back, causing him to fall into the bread rack."

.   .   .

I remember the first time an officer I worked with used his weapon in the line of duty. I was off duty at the time, but I learned what happened later. The officers were given information that a wanted, possibly armed suspect was in the general area of northwest La Grande. One of the officers patrolling the area spotted the suspect, wearing a leather jacket, in an alley and called out to him. He ran away with his hands out of the officer's sight. The officer followed him, shouting at him to stop and show his hands. The officer drew his firearm, and as soon as the suspect stopped and turned, the officer focused on the suspect's hands. He said it was like a slow-motion movie: he clearly saw the handgun as the suspect raised it toward the officer, and without thinking, the officer fired three times and the suspect fell to the ground. All three rounds struck the suspect's abdomen surprisingly not killing him. I learned an interesting fact about what happens when hollow-point bullets strike a leather jacket. The hollow point fills and responds like any ball ammo, so instead of expanding like a hollow-point round is intended to, it will go directly through the target and leave an exit hole the same size as the entry hole. During the suspect's attempted-murder trial, the defense argued that size of the exit holes indicated that the officer actually shot the suspect in the back. However, the jury saw past this and found him guilty. There was a lot of media interest and subsequent community interest in this officer-involved shooting, and I found it interesting that along with this attention came increased support and appreciation for the police department and its officers.

. . .

In 1988, the department had an opening for the position of corporal, so I applied and brushed up on laws, policies, and procedures. I received the promotion and was assigned to an experienced sergeant's team. The corporal worked Tuesday through Thursday with the sergeant and then worked alone Friday and Saturday, so the only days I really had any responsibility were the busiest days of the week.

On one particular Friday night, I responded to a medical-assist call. An elderly woman was reported down on a driveway just a few blocks away from me, and I was there in under a minute. The woman was having a heart attack, and I quickly started CPR. When a second officer arrived, we performed two-man CPR until the ambulance arrived.

I'm not sure why the ambulance was so short staffed, but the medic was the only person in the ambulance, so as the corporal, I decided to have the other officer drive the ambulance so the medic could continue CPR. The hospital was less than two miles away, so I told him to just drive safely and get there. He did. The medic called me later that night to tell me how much he appreciated our help, and he gave me the good news that the woman was alive. The other officer and I were so pleased with our save, but we were brought back to reality as soon as the sergeant learned that I had told the officer to drive the ambulance. He did not say one word of praise about the save but rather focused on the high risk of liability we assumed. I was later rewarded by being allowed to speak with this victim. This woman came into the police station to report a theft. She said that while she had been in the hospital, some of her family had helped themselves to her property. Although it was sad that this woman had family who had taken advantage of her, I took pride in knowing, because of my actions, she was able to make the report.

. . .

That same sergeant later resigned under a cloud of complaints of his excessive use of force. One of them came after I made a burglary arrest when the suspect resisted. I got the suspect to the jail and was across the book-in counter from him when he suddenly grabbed a phone and reared back like he was going to throw it at me. The corrections deputy who was standing next to him reached across the suspect's face to grab the phone, and the suspect bit the deputy's forearm. The suspect, a man who stood no more than five foot six inches, and my sergeant, who was at least six foot three inches, then went into the interview room. When they came out a short time later, the suspect had a bloody nose. The interview room also had blood smears on the walls about six feet from the floor. I didn't have to be a detective to know what happened in there.

. . .

A second incident occurred after I observed a hit-and-run accident. I was less than a block away from a vehicle that ran a red light and broadsided a second vehicle. The driver of the first vehicle, a white male, sped away, and I pursued to a residential area, where the vehicle pulled in behind a two-story house. The sergeant was close by, and he went to the back of the house while I, with the aid of dispatcher, called in to the house. While in the process of having dispatch speak with an occupant of the home, I heard a commotion at the back of the house. I ran over. The sergeant had tackled a man as he left the house and had him in handcuffs and facedown in the yard. My immediate thought was that I wasn't sure this was the driver. I scolded the man, and he reacted like a child who had done something wrong, not defiantly like someone being falsely accused. I softened my approach and asked, "Didn't you see me?" He said no and added that he was sorry. The sergeant took the suspect to my car while I talked with a second man who had come outside. When I got back to my patrol car, there was a dent in my trunk with a blood smear on it, and the suspect had a bloody nose. This was the final straw for the sergeant.

Chapter Five

La Grande Investigations

During my time on patrol, I had always conducted my own investigations and put a great deal of effort into helping other officers with their cases. I even volunteered to take on the not-so-popular non-sufficient funds check crimes, thinking this might be an avenue into detective work. I was right. In 1989, I was assigned as the department's detective. The agency was very good about getting me into relevant training. Early on, I received training in Interviewing techniques, homicide investigations, and use of the Identi-Kit (for creating composite pictures of suspects), all of which would prove extremely valuable.

During the first week of my investigations career I was called out to assist the outgoing detective with an assault case. We had a midforties woman, who lived with her young-adult daughter, and who, while sleeping, had her head severely beaten. She was now at the hospital in a coma. The assault had taken place in the single mother's bed and there was a large amount of blood on the sheets, pillow and headboard. On the floor lay an aluminum baseball bat, so it was logical that we had our weapon.

The house was searched and we found a pair of men's tennis shoes on the back porch, just at the entry to the kitchen. No other items appeared to be of evidentiary value. The crime lab was called in and they took over the scene while I began following-up with interviews. The daughter spoke about her concern that her boyfriend may have been involved and explained that her mother was against their relationship and was not afraid to tell him. She also said that her mother had learned of his drug use and, the daughter believed, her mom would have reported this activity to his probation officer.

The daughter did not recognize the shoes or the aluminum bat, however she said she knew her boyfriend played softball and also believed he did have an aluminum bat. She added that she just never paid any attention to the bat so she couldn't tell us if this was or was not his bat.

During this time we did not have the luxury of sending our evidence off, such as the shoes, and asking for DNA evidence, but what we did try and do was collect hairs and fibers from inside those shoes in hopes of finding a match on our suspect or in his home. We also were unfortunate to learn that the aluminum bat revealed no fingerprints and, because of the coating on the bat, it did not even show any traces of blood from our victim.

We obtained consent from the boyfriend to search his apartment and we did find some carpet fibers that appeared, and were later classified similar but not conclusive, to those found in the shoes. We also learned that the size of the found shoes were the same as our newly-developed suspect. Our suspect denied any knowledge of the assault and he said that he did not own an aluminum bat, adding, when confronted about being seen using one, that he just used his teammates bat. Other teammates were contacted and they confirmed our suspect did have his own aluminum bat and their description matched the one we now had in evidence. I searched the dumpster, at our suspect's apartment, and on top of the garbage was a soiled pair of white sox. Fibers from these sox were also shipped off to the crime lab and we later learned that they were also similar but not conclusive, to some found in the shoes.

Our suspect, during the interview by the other detective, continued to deny any involvement and our only option appeared to be to turn the information over to his probation officer. Our suspect was then arrested for drug use and violating his probation.

Our victim recovered but had no memory of the assault. The other detective had been through an advanced interrogation school and, believing we had nothing to lose; he used the study of biorhythms to pick an interview time that he believed our suspect would be at his most vulnerable. Immediately after the interview I received the detective's call telling me he had obtained a full confession. Our suspect admitted that he did not like the interference from his girlfriend's mother. He also believed that she was going to turn him in for drug use so during the middle of the night he snuck over, taking off his shoes so he would make as little noise as possible, and then beat his victim with the bat. After the assault he panicked, leaving his bat and shoes behind then running, in just his sox, back to his apartment.

. . .

The entire time I envisioned becoming a detective, I never stopped to think about the negatives. During this time, the state of Oregon was pushing for higher standards in child-abuse investigations, and I soon found myself as the primary contact for all abuse complaints. I was quick to learn that for these sensitive cases, I needed all the compassion I could muster but I also had to develop a poker face so I wouldn't influence what the child or suspect might say. I knew how much I disliked testifying and could only imagine how bad it would be for a child or a battered woman. I realized that our justice system could further traumatize the victims and that the best way to avoid this was to obtain a confession and ultimately a guilty plea from the perpetrator. Interviewing with goal of getting a confession soon became my passion.

One case stands out from the others throughout the years. It was my first abuse case that went to trial. A handicapped girl had reported being fondled by her mother's boyfriend. I interviewed the girl and followed up with an interview of the boyfriend. I felt good that I got him to change his story from his never having any contact to his statement that maybe he accidentally touched her vaginal area while he applied lotion. I recorded this interview and believe now that I backed off the interrogation too early. In court, I was allowed to play the recording of his changing story. The prosecutor asked a question to highlight the change. The defense attorney objected, saying the question had already been asked and answered during the playing of the tape recording. The judge sustained it, and the Jury was not able to hear any further comments about his statement. The verdict of not guilty has stuck with me. A few weeks after the trial, I was sitting alone on my front porch when the defense attorney happened by. He stopped and talked with me, and he told me he thought I had done a good job with the investigation. He hoped that I wouldn't be discouraged by the results. He also said that his job was to provide the best defense, regardless what he thought of the defendant. I think he meant to emphasize this last point, but it did help to hear some encouraging words.

.   .   .

In another case, a handicapped woman went into a small clinic in an adjacent town to report being raped by a male ER nurse who worked at the La Grande hospital. I interviewed the woman, and although too much time had elapsed between rape and examination to find seminal fluid, I found her story credible and knew she had been forced to have sex. My anxiety increased as I contemplated how I could ever get a "respected professional" to admit that he would rape anyone, let alone a disabled person. I conducted the interview and locked him into the statement that he had met the woman when she had visited the ER for assistance with a chronic migraine. He said that he had followed up by visiting her home later that night, but only to check on her condition.

Besides the sex, the only glaring difference between their statements was that he said he had entered through the front door, while she said he had entered, without knocking, through the back door. I asked him the only bait question I could think of: "Would there be any reason why your shoe prints would be found in the mud at the back door?" He immediately changed his answer, just like most other guilty people do. He now said that he had seen the light on at the back of the house and assumed that was the house's primary entrance. I then relentlessly shot one theme after another at him.

He listened, not denying, until I finally hit a theme that she may have been highly sexualized and that, without even thinking about it, he responded to her advances. Once he admitted that there was "consensual sex," I questioned him further about how he thought society would view his behavior. I approached him with the idea that our culture draws an imaginary line between acceptable behavior and unacceptable behavior. I asked how he thought the general public would view his behavior, and he admitted that he had crossed the line into unacceptable behavior. He later entered a guilty plea on second-degree rape.

·　·　·

There was a rash of headstone tippings in our local cemetery. The damage was extensive, but with little evidence to go on, the case was turned over to investigations. I talked with some local youths, trying to gain confidential statements of who they thought could be responsible, assuring those who spoke that nothing would be traced back to them. A group of youths stood out to them as capable of performing such meaningless crimes: part of the Dungeons & Dragons club.

After several interviews, I had narrowed down the list of club members, and during interviews, with those members, they admitted that their acts started as dares during a club meeting. The part that was most disturbing, and that I hadn't known until these interviews, was that they had gained entry to a sealed crypt to lie with the deceased as part of the dare. I further learned that one of the members had removed a ring finger from the deceased. I immediately interrogated that teen and obtained a confession. When I asked where the finger was, the teen told me that it was missing and believed to have been eaten by a dog.

·　·　·

In 1987, my wife and I were blessed with the birth of our daughter, and in February 1990, we had a son. During the delivery of our son, my wife was next to another woman giving birth who yelled and even threw things at the nurses, demanding painkillers. The nurses were so appreciative of my wife and just rolled their eyes at the other woman's behavior. That day, both women gave birth to boys.

About three months later, I was called to a residence to investigate a domestic between father and daughter. This was the house of the boy who was born on the same day as my son and the dispute was between his mother and her dad. I found him laying in a car seat in the corner of the living room. The mother and grandfather both sat at the kitchen table smoking, and very little attention appeared to be given to the boy. The next I heard about this child was in August of that same year and was from another detective who, after I returned from vacation, told me that he had investigated the child's death. The death was ruled a case of sudden infant death syndrome. I couldn't help but think about that life and how he and my son were born to such different families and how unfair it was that this boy's life had to end so abruptly.

.   .   .

Around this same time, La Grande had a string of robberies in which women's purses were grabbed by an unknown suspect on a motorcycle. We also had a rash of gropings, Peeping Toms, and undergarment thefts. These crimes scared the community and placed a lot of pressure on both me and the department to solve them. The college even brought in Laura X, an advocate for female victims of domestic violence who had been on the TV show *60 Minutes*. I was selected to participate as a panel member in a public forum at our college auditorium for a discussion of local issues, and I remember with agony the dissatisfaction directed at me and the La Grande Police Department. Someone in the media asked if one of the victims of the groper had been injured. I clearly answered that there was no physical injury but that I was sure the victim suffered emotional trauma. Of course, what hit the paper was, "Detective States Woman Not Injured."

We tried to set up surveillance in the areas where the purse snatchings and gropings were occurring, but with the irregularity of occurrences and inconsistent pattern to their locations, we weren't having much luck. From a more general location, southwest La Grande, or close to Morgan Lake Road, we were receiving calls of prowlers and undergarment thefts. We had a voice-activated radio-dispatched (VARDA) alarm, which, when activated by pressure, would send out the signal "You have an alarm at target x" over the police frequency. We set this up under windows of some of the women's houses, including the home of a female police officer. She had previously reported seeing a prowler, hearing noises, and experiencing other circumstances that left her knowing someone was watching her.

In this same time frame, a pharmacy in southwest La Grande repeatedly reported thefts of prescription medication. The pharmacy owner told us that there appeared to be some damage to the store's outer lock but that the interior building and cabinet locks were never damaged. The pharmacy owner had done an inventory and found a large amount of painkillers missing. The owner had thought that maybe an employee or a previous employee could be responsible. Although the outside lock had been rekeyed, the employee could still have a key for the inner locks and so would only have to break the outside lock to gain access. The owner offered to help us by setting up surveillance equipment.

Then a call came in from the pharmacy owner, who said he had again found the back lock tampered with. In a review of the surveillance tape, he saw the subject gain entry and steal drugs. We responded and collected the videotape. The man on the tape was easily identified by the pharmacy owner and other officers as a man who lived near the pharmacy. Even more interesting was that he lived just a few houses away from where our Morgan Lake victim had been living at the time of her murder. In the video the suspect was wearing an identifiable ball cap, and after obtaining a search warrant, we went to his home. He answered the door wearing the same ball cap as in the video. Another officer took him away for an interview while I participated in the search.

He had prescription medication throughout his bedroom but of more interest were the dozens of women's purses and hundreds of bras and pairs of panties lying around. My team immediately secured the residence and modified the search warrant to include the crimes of robbery, residential burglary, theft, and trespass. In the purses, we found IDs of most of the women who had had their purses snatched and many who had never reported a theft. We also found dozens of Polaroid photos of our suspect wearing only women's undergarments. The size of the cache of panties and bras indicated this was something that had been going on for years. (The female officer and a dispatcher later identified some of our seized undergarments as belonging to them.)

The suspect refused to admit he was the one in the video even after he viewed it and could see that at the time of the crime he was wearing the same hat that he had been arrested in. Despite this, there was more than enough evidence to send him away for a long time.

The district attorney worked a plea deal I believe to a couple counts each of robbery and burglary with the remainder uncharged if he cooperated fully in an interview. I jumped at the opportunity.

It started off simple enough as we went through the pharmacy break-ins. He said he had gotten the idea after breaking into the home of a pharmacy employee and stealing her purse and keys. He mentioned the changed exterior lock but unchanged interior locks. He listed each time he made entry, stating that at first he tried to take small quantities of drugs but after being successful, he got greedy.

I talked with him about the purse snatchings, and he said that he just found it to be an easy way to steal purses. I then asked about his peeping and thefts of undergarments. This was when the hair stood up on the back of my neck. I suggested that he might have looked for easy opportunities, such as laundry on a line or homes left unlocked while people were away. He said no, the thrill for him was to be in the home with the women when they didn't know he was there. He said that while the women were showering or sleeping, he would try to get as close to them as he could and then take the undergarments as souvenirs. I asked him to tell me where these break-ins and peepings had taken place, and he confessed to crimes well beyond the southeast part of La Grande. He explained that he had spent a lot of his time around college apartments and that he had even gone into the nearby community of Union.

He told me that the gropings were just a progression of his desire to get as close to women as he could and that they gave him a sexual high and a feeling of power. He would not admit to any unreported more serious crime, of rape or murder; however, that didn't stop me from thinking about the possibility of his being connected to our Morgan Lake murder.

.   .   .

In the early evening of a night off, I was called out to conduct a death investigation at an apartment. Neighbors told officers that they had not seen their neighbor in several days, and the landlord agreed to unlock the door for the officers who then called me in.

When I arrived, I found what looked like a scene from a horror movie. There was blood on the carpet in the entryway, and to the left on the kitchen floor were a large amount of blood smears. It appeared that someone had tried to wipe up the blood from the kitchen floor but quit before finishing. Blood was smeared on the walls, about waist high, throughout the house. The deceased was on the bathroom floor with a large wound to the back of his head. The toilet seat was up and inside the bowl was vomit.

The scene was almost overwhelming, and my mind started racing to come up with an idea of who could have done something like this. We called out the crime lab, and I sketched the scene, trying to record every blood smear and pool. I noticed several empty bottles of booze in the victim's wastebasket. About an hour into my investigation, I started putting the pieces together. The man lived alone and the house was locked. There were signs that the deceased was drinking to excess, and the kitchen floor indicated that someone had tried to clean up the blood. The victim had obviously been bleeding for some time, so had this been an assault, he would have had more than enough time to call for help. This told me that only the deceased, who was the only person living there, could be responsible for this attempt to clean the floor. By the time the crime lab arrived, I had located a clump of the deceased's hair and blood on the nightstand.

The crime lab also believed that the deceased had fallen into the nightstand and started bleeding. Maybe because of his elevated blood-alcohol level, his body could not stop the blood flow. He got sick and ultimately died alone.

. . .

During my tenure as a detective, I was assigned as the department's representative to the Oregon Together committee, part of a state-wide approach to reduce alcohol and drug use by our youth, with representatives from schools, businesses, and the juvenile department. During one of our meetings, increased activity associated with gangs came up. This activity had no known ties to any of the Southern California gangs, but schools and businesses were reporting young men hanging out together wearing gang colors, with a specific group wearing ball caps with "VLT" on them.

While researching gangs and the law enforcement's approach to them, I found that we needed to stop and talk with the youth and ask them who they were and what they were up to. A larger agency was using this tactic, and its members claimed it was the best way to discourage criminal activity. The idea was to make an effort to just stop and talk with these youths where they were hanging out and to document their names, nick-names, and descriptions of their clothing. They also stressed the importance of documenting the gangs' associations with any criminal charges.

The chief and the rest of the committee agreed with this approach, so the school district enacted policies to limit gang-related clothing or hats on school grounds. It wasn't long before I was facing complaints from several parents who believed we were harassing their "angels." I received information from informants about the VLT's activity in petty thefts, including one case in which members had repeatedly threatened a man with violence if he didn't give them cash and cigarettes.

I approached this man, who was mentally handicapped and yet because of a "life skills" program was able to live alone, and he said he had not reported the acts because he hadn't wanted to make waves or face retaliation from the gang. He acknowledged that members of the VLT's regularly approached him or telephoned him demanding money, cigarettes, or both. I asked him if I could place a recorder on his phone (in Oregon, we only needed his consent to record any call), and he agreed. Within a few days, he called me back to say that the gang had called him, and they told him they would beat him up if he didn't give them more money. I went to his home and listened to the tape. It couldn't have been any better. The key organizer of the VLTs, one of the "angels" whose parents had made threats to sue if we didn't quit harassing their son, was the caller, and his words rang out clearly: "I will have my gang beat you up unless you give me more money." The victim provided names and descriptions of the other four gang members, and in no time at all, we had all five in custody on gang-enhanced robbery charges.

I interviewed the "angel" and obtained a taped confession, which included him telling me the gang's name was Vatos Locos Teenagers. I called his parents and asked that they come to the police station, and they did. When I met them in the lobby, they were fired up at my ongoing harassment of their son. I had the tape recorder in my hand and wasted no time in playing the clip of their son's confession in which he said he had been using his gang as a threat to gain cash for them. This and other arrests of gang members stemmed all gang activity and the wearing of gang clothing or colors at schools and in the community.

.   .   .

La Grande sometimes went through fads of criminal activity. During one four-week period, we had a rash of vandalism to businesses' windows, which were broken by BB guns. Nothing motivates a chief more than a group of business owners at a city council meeting questioning what the agency was doing about the vandalism. We had noticed that most of the damage occurred on Friday and Saturday nights, so we targeted groups of young men driving around together late at night. On one of these focused stops, officers saw BBs on the floor of a car carrying four youths. They consented to a search, which revealed several CO2 pistols. After that, it wasn't long before the youths confessed to the vandalism.

Shortly after this activity stopped, we experienced a series of pipe-bomb explosions. Mailboxes all over town were blown up, and eventually the high school library's window was blown out. Those who thought not enough was being done to stop this activity again requested we step up our investigations. Fortunately, informants provided the names of three youths who they believed were involved. The primary suspect was the son of a plumber. (Who better to have the supplies necessary for such activity?) We pulled the youths in for interviews, but they initially denied us any confessions. Our next step was to contact their parents and explain our concerns in an effort to gain their cooperation. I contacted one of the parents, who denied consent to search their home, and she gave me the common parental line, "It couldn't be my child." Within a half hour after I left this home, the mother called me. She had been concerned enough by my beliefs that she checked her son's room and found several homemade pipe bombs in his dresser.

At that time, our bomb-disposal procedure was to remove a bomb and transport it to our rural weapons range, where we would lock it up until the bomb team from western Oregon arrived to detonate it. I returned to the home and I collected the bombs, placed them in the trunk of my car, and drove them to the range. The youth's were arrested and, with their bombs now in our possession, they confessed.

.   .   .

Many officers called me lucky and gifted when it came to interviews. Some even went as far as saying that if they were ever accused of any wrongdoing, they would not allow me to interview them. I recall one such lucky case, an armed robbery of our only liquor store. A man in his early to midtwenties with blond hair and wearing camouflage fatigues forced the clerk into the back room and handcuffed her to a desk. He struck her in the head with a bottle before he gathered cash and several bottles of booze and headed out the door.

After I was called to the scene, I canvassed the area, and I found camouflage clothing tossed behind the nearby post office. While collecting them, I noticed an unusually strong smell of cigarette smoke. I later completed an Identi-Kit composite of our suspect but soon ran out of leads. One afternoon, I was walking by the open door of the interview room and noticed an officer interviewing a man about a criminal-mischief report. I thought of how unusually strong the cigarette odor coming from that interview room was. I pulled the officer out to speak with him, and I asked; "Can you humor me and show the subject you are speaking to the Identi-Kit composite and camouflage clothing from our liquor store robbery?" He asked "Why?" I paused then said; "Because of the strong cigarette smell coming from your guy." "You're crazy." He replied. That's right—I had a hunch only because of the smell.

The officer did humor me, however, and what a surprise. The subject thought the composite looked like his roommate and said the pants definitely belonged to his roommate, and he supported this belief by pointing out some snags on the bottom of the pants, caused by his cat's using his roommate's leg as a claw sharpener. We picked up the roommate, and I obtained a full confession. The officer suggested that I keep what led me to him a secret.

. . .

In another interesting case, at four in the morning, a motel employee called in an armed robbery. She reported that a masked intruder had entered the office, pointed a stainless-steel revolver at her, and demanded all of the cash. This was on the east end of La Grande and across from another motel and a restaurant that would not be open until six. I didn't believe I would be able to locate any witnesses.

I found checks and receipts tossed on the ground next to the motel, leaving about $250 in cash unaccounted for. The motel had a mercury light above the entrance, and the main portion of the door was glass. When I talked with the clerk, she said that the suspect had rung the night bell, and she had made her way from her bedroom into the adjacent office and then used the door release at the desk to allow the suspect in. He took the contents of the cash box and immediately left. As I spoke with her, the motel owner arrived, and the clerk was receiving the attention, from her family and the motel owner, that was expected for someone who had been through such a trauma. I told her that I may need to contact her later, and she said that would be fine.

I returned to my office and started thinking about how unusual it would be for the suspect to take the time to clear out the cash box while he was still next to the motel. I also found it hard to believe that the clerk, who would have had a clear view of anyone standing at the entrance because of the glass door and mercury light, would have pushed the button to let a masked man enter.

My anxieties increased. I knew the clerk was not being honest with me, but I also knew that she was receiving lots of attention because of this crime, and under those circumstances, it would be hard for anyone to admit they had lied about being robbed. My dilemma was to gain her cooperation and catch her in a lie without being labeled as an insensitive, overly aggressive detective.

I called the clerk and told her that I had received a call from a logger who had been sitting with other crew members in a crummy (a five passenger pick-up truck) in the parking lot of the restaurant across the street waiting for their last crew member. They had arrived at 3:30 a.m. and departed at 4:05 a.m., just after the police arrived. The logger told me that when he saw the police arrive, he wondered what had taken place. I told him I appreciated his call and explained that there had been a robbery. I then asked him what he remembered about the man entering the motel at about four that morning. To my surprise, he had a clear view of the motel and said no one had gone in. I asked my alleged robbery victim if it was possible that the robbery had not occurred at four o'clock, as she had reported, but rather prior to three thirty, when the logger arrived. She hesitated, her "hmms" and "ahs" after I asked the question was a clear indication of someone caught in a lie. She responded in a way that only a guilty person would. She said, "You know, now that I've had a chance to think about it, I may have gone to the bathroom first then thought about it for a bit before calling 911." I said I had a few more questions and asked that she meet me at the police department.

She arrived as scheduled, and I now had the confidence to interrogate her. Just a few minutes into the questioning, I could see she was ready to break down and cry. I opened with a theme about her needing money, and she explained that she had medical issues and a growing list of bills. It was not long before she pulled the cash from her purse and wanted to make sure it was all returned to the motel owners. She did lose her job, and she pleaded guilty to theft and initiating a false police report, but in confessing, she seemed to gain some sense of pride in herself for doing the right thing. When I explained to another officer (the same who had called me crazy when trusting my sense of smell) that I had told her about the loggers waiting for their crew member, he stopped me and wanted to know who the logger was, adding that he spent many years working in the woods. I felt bad when I had to tell him I had made that up.

·   ·   ·

Our town went through a period where our businesses were being regularly burglarized. The burglar's modus operandi was to break in, rummage around, find the cash box, and get out. Seven businesses were hit one night. Early the next morning, I went to each of these businesses to get anything that might help me solve this case. Once again an odor stood out, this time strong body odor. I also found that several of the businesses reported a large amount of coins missing from their petty cash boxes.

I returned to my office and called local motels to ask the night clerks if anyone had checked in late, if anyone had paid for a room in coins, and if anyone who checked in had a strong body odor. On about my third call, the clerk answered yes to all three of these questions. We responded to the suspect's room, and I went to the front door while a second officer went to the back window. Who would have guessed that as soon as I knocked and announced myself at the front door, the back window would have opened? He was caught and he knew it. He gave a full confession.

.   .   .

We had a series of car-stereo thefts and residential burglaries in which stereos, tools, and cash were stolen. I received enough information on a suspect and residence that I was able to get a search warrant. While executing the warrant, I told the suspect that we were looking for stolen items from some car clouts and a burglary. I asked him if he had any knowledge of the thefts or break-ins, and he said no. I asked him if he had ever been in the home that was burglarized, and he again said no.

In the suspect's house, we found a shelf full of car and home stereos; it looked like the appliance section of a secondhand store. Midway through our search, I saw a stereo that I believed to have come from the residential burglary. I said sarcastically, "Look what we have here," I asked the suspect where it came from. He said that a friend had brought it by and, seeing my skepticism, added that this was a different model from the one stolen in that burglary. I paused, looked back at him, and asked, "How would you know that?" He responded, "I don't have to talk to you." I checked the report and found that he was correct—this was the same brand but a different model. Nonetheless, this stereo turned out to have been stolen in another burglary. Later in the search, I found a cache of tools in the attic crawl space. I asked if he knew about these tools, and he said he knew nothing about them. I suggested that they were also stolen, and he immediately responded, "They didn't come from that burglary." Once again I asked, "How would you know that?" He said again that he didn't have to answer that question.

The case ended up going to trial, and I enjoyed relaying his statements to the jury. He was convicted, and in passing, I talked with his attorney. He said that he wished his clients would just keep their mouths shut, adding that at the end of his career, he wanted to write a book about stupid statements and would definitely include this guy's in it.

. . .

I was fortunate to be able to attend a stress-management class for police officers held in nearby Pendleton, Oregon. The instructor provided a great deal of information and research about the health hazards of police work, specifically stress and its effects on the human body. He described that each person's biological flow, or reaction to high levels of stress, rises from close to normal to extreme levels during times of danger. This means every time an officer goes to work, his system goes into overdrive. The problem with this is that the body needs an equal amount of recovery time to level out again, but a drop from such an elevated state was not normal for people, and this causes depression and a lack of willingness for officers to do anything during their off duty time. He also brought up the problem of officers getting together at this time when their bodies need to recover. They tend to tell stories of a recent pursuit or arrest, which gives them an adrenaline rush just like they were back on duty, and the body once again becomes hypersensitive. I now realized the importance of my woodworking, photography, and family time and also how unhealthy it was to listen to the police scanner when not at work.

. . .

In 1991, I was working as acting sergeant over investigations, and two other detectives worked in the division. The chief received permission to promote another sergeant and make the position permanent. I applied but was not selected. Immediately after the new sergeant was installed, I returned to patrol.

Back on patrol, I was assigned to work a shift with another corporal. It was winter and had recently snowed, so the roads were still icy. Around one thirty in the morning, we received a cluster of reports of windows smashed on vehicles parked along our main roads. Because of the visibility of these damaged vehicles, I knew that the crimes had just occurred. I told the other corporal that we should split up and look for an open-bed pickup with at least two individuals inside. He asked how I could so quickly arrive at this conclusion, and I told him that the damage appeared to have been caused by a large chain: it occurred on the driver's side of the parked vehicles, and there was rust left behind on the damaged glass. For the chain to be that rusty, I concluded that it would have been in an open-bed pickup, where it was always exposed to the rain and snow. Since the damage was on the driver's side of the parked vehicles, someone on the passenger's side of the suspect's vehicle would have been the one swinging the chain.

We split up, and the first pickup I passed had two occupants. I found a reason to stop them, and as I approached, I saw a large chain, on top of the recent snow, in the pickup's bed. Before even talking with the occupants, I called for the other corporal to respond. To separate the two subjects, I placed one in the back of my patrol car, and I had the second step out onto the sidewalk in front of me. I asked his permission to search the chain, and I retrieved tweezers and envelopes from my trunk. I put gloves on and then lifted the chain from the truck bed and placed it on the ground between the truck and my headlights, where both subjects could see what I was doing. I looked it over and then picked out a couple of small ice chunks to put into the envelopes. At about this time the other corporal arrived and listened as I questioned each subject about his activity, throwing in the bait question, "Would there be any reason glass collected off of your chain would match glass from our victims' vehicles?" Both subjects were quick to confess and say that they were just being stupid. I ended up citing them for all of the vandalism. The other corporal let me know up front that I was never to question him about anything.

.   .   .

The two of us had another exciting moment during one of La Grande's many bar brawls. The barmaid stepped in to break the fight up, and one of the assailants turned and stabbed her. She said she never even saw the knife. As we waited for the ambulance, bystanders gave us a basic description of the stabber and the direction he had fled. I started down the alley, where he was last seen, and I saw lights on in the apartment above a business. At the apartment's entrance, I noticed a small amount of blood near the doorframe. The other corporal and I quickly got cover from the county and state police and challenged the occupants of the lit room. Lo and behold, the suspect surrendered. It wasn't until we had him in cuffs that we knew who he was. A records check then revealed that he was out of California, where he had an outstanding murder warrant.

. . .

On April 8, 1992, in John Day, another Eastern Oregon community, the officer on duty, Frank Ward, responded to a domestic dispute. Frank, who was five feet ten inches and of average build, met with a six-foot-five-inch, two-hundred-twenty-five-pound logger. Frank was killed by repeated blows to the head from a block of wood. I had never met Frank, but several officers at La Grande Police Department had, and they told me he was a great guy. He was thirty-nine years old and had a wife, daughter, and twin two-year-old sons. I was one of a handful of La Grande officers who attended Frank's funeral. We wore our dress uniforms and were greeted by an honor guard and a lone bagpipe player. I sat about ten rows behind Frank's wife and children. I tried hard to live up to the tough image of a police officer, but when I saw the mother and children huddling in pain during George Strait's song "A Fathers Love," I could no longer control the pain that I was feeling or control my tears for someone who was only a brother in law enforcement.

Chapter Six

Deschutes County Sheriff's Office Patrol

In the fall of 1992, I saw a listing for a job in Deschutes County. This was the area where my wife was raised and most of her family still lived. I asked if she wanted me to apply, and she thought it might be good for us to see where the process took us. I wasn't sure that I wanted to move, but I decided to go through the motions. If I were offered a job, great, but if not, I had lost nothing. I submitted my application, including answers to four questions in a two-page handwritten response. I was then invited to take the written test. I arrived at Central Oregon Community College and was amazed at the long line of applicants. We provided identification and were led into a commons area with about one hundred tables, each set up for four applicants. The lieutenant got up and thanked everyone for their interest in this position. He confirmed that four hundred applicants had been invited to take the written test but said that only one hundred would receive an invitation to take the physical fitness portion. I realized that Deschutes County must be a desirable location if there were this many applicants and that I wanted this job. I went from not caring to being highly motivated and focused on obtaining a score in the top 25 percent. I looked at the other three candidates seated at my table and thought, *I have to beat your scores.*

I received notice that I had passed with a 92 percent and was invited to take the fitness portion. The fitness test came and went, and next up was the interview. I felt good as I left the panel of four, and I later learned that if they had had the authority, they would have issued me a uniform right then.

On February 1, 1993, five other deputies and I began our careers with the Deschutes County Sheriff's Office. Deschutes County is located in Central Oregon and at that time had a population under ninety thousand. It is known for its abundance of sunshine and blue skies, mountains, lakes, and skiing at Mount Bachelor. The sheriff's office had four patrol teams, each with a sergeant and six deputies. We worked twelve-hour shifts: two days 6:00 a.m. to 6:00 p.m., two nights 6:00 p.m. to 6:00 a.m. Then we had four days off.

After I spent a couple of weeks with a training officer the sergeant wanted to ride with me to complete his own evaluation. We stopped to cover an experienced deputy on a suspected DUI, and saw that the driver had rolled up his window, locked his door, and would not respond to any of the deputy's commands. The sergeant positioned himself next to the deputy, and I went to the passenger's side of the car. The deputy pulled out his baton and demanded that the driver open the door. I had a quick flashback to the rolled-over van, with the medics opening the back doors and simply walking in. I looked down at the passenger's door, opened it, and got in. Once inside the car, I took the keys out of the ignition and told the driver to exit the car. He did. The sergeant looked at me with a smile and said, "I guess you did things differently in La Grande." I didn't respond, but this lesson actually came from Boardman.

Shortly afterward, the sergeant and I stopped our own suspected DUI, and after I arrested the driver, we took her into our booking room to give her an Intoxilyzer test. The sergeant stood behind me, and I stood in the doorway next to the Intoxilyzer, with the woman in front of me and facing me and the sergeant. I had placed a mouthpiece on the instrument and given the woman instructions for blowing into it. Once I instructed her to blow, she grabbed the mouthpiece with both hands, dropped to her knees, and pretended like she was blowing into the tube. I knew she was trying to trick the machine, so I simplified the instructions, saying, "You need to blow," "Blow harder," and "Keep blowing." The sergeant was laughing uncontrollably. I didn't let him distract me, and I obtained an adequate breath sample. Then I realized what this looked and sounded like from the sergeant's position. The sergeant added that in his twenty-plus years, he had never seen anyone drop to their knees in front of the deputy and use both hands on the tube like that, and my instructions added to his enjoyment, making this too much for him to handle. He gave his blessing for me to begin solo duties.

. . .

I was initially assigned as the team traffic deputy, which meant I would rotate districts and focus on traffic violations and accidents. One of the first major accidents happened in July just south of La Pine. It involved a southbound pickup carrying eight migrant workers returning from the Washington apple harvest and a northbound semitruck. The semitruck blew a stop sign, and the pickup crashed into the trailer's side. When I was on my way to the scene, I heard the desperation in the unusually high pitch of the first arriving deputy as he asked me where I was. I knew it was bad. It was hard to grasp that of the eight family members in the pickup, only three remained alive.

Before all of the bodies were covered cars were passing and slowed down so the drivers could get a better look. The initial deputy lost it and screamed at one of the passing motorists. Although he may not have been politically correct, he was right to do what he did. If the motorists had seen the extent of the injuries—one passenger's head had almost been severed from his body—they would have known the evil side of curiosity and would think twice before gawking the next time they passed an accident.

. . .

I was lucky to have had three years' experience as a La Grande detective, and it enabled me, and gave me the responsibility, to assist the other new deputies on a lot of the sex-abuse calls we received. One such call, a sixteen-year-old reporting an attempted abuse, went out to one of our brand-new deputies. I offered to assist, and he was appreciative. We first talked with the girl, and she explained that she had gone to a business in Bend and was going to wait for her father to pick her up. The business owner, who knew her family, offered to give her a ride home, which she accepted. On the way home, he asked her to give him a blow job and offered her fifty dollars if she would do it. She declined, and as soon as her father arrived home, she told him what had happened.

The other deputy and I went to the business, and I asked the owner if he would talk with us. He agreed, and we went outside behind the business. The owner was initially adamant that nothing had happened and that he would never have made such a request. I told him that it was obvious he had a track record for making good decisions; otherwise he wouldn't have a business. I went into a theme about how at one time or another all people do something stupid that they later regret. I added that I kind of hoped this was one of those occasions. I told him I would often meet people who were good people who made a mistake. I told him I felt good when those people are confronted about their mistakes and they then admit their wrongdoing and accept the consequences. I assured him that I didn't think of him as someone who always did wrong and that I thought this was a one-time mistake. I also added that I hoped I would be able to leave him with just a citation to appear in court, knowing that he was an upstanding citizen who would be willing to make his court appearance.

He then told us that he didn't know why it happened, but he admitted that he had asked the girl for oral sex and, knowing that she was at an age where she needed money, he offered to give her fifty dollars. I thanked him for being honest and left him with a citation to appear for the crime of soliciting prostitution. The district attorney said that to his knowledge, my citation was the first of its kind in Deschutes County. I had to go to court on a motion to suppress, the defense attorney's effort to get the crime thrown out, with the reasoning that I had used unacceptable practices to gain a confession.

In court, the defense attorney laid out his argument that I was armed with a gun and handcuffs and thus by my presence had coerced a confession from his client. He also threw in that I was nice to the defendant and therefore was trying to gain an incriminating statement even before I had advised him of his rights. The judge seemed a little confused and repeated the defense attorney's claims:

"You have a uniformed deputy carrying a handgun and handcuffs and a deputy who is nice." The attorney agreed with the simplification but cited a few remotely similar cases to strengthen his argument, but the judge simply said, "I don't know where you're from, but here in Deschutes County, we expect our officers to be armed and nice." He ruled that this argument would not be a basis for throwing out a case in his courtroom.

.   .   .

Friday—and Saturday-night shifts were always the busiest and the ones that caused me the greatest preshift anxiety. Not knowing what lay ahead along with the knowledge of just how busy Fridays and Saturdays were gave me a unique mix of anticipation and uneasy tension.

This Friday night our team was short the northwest deputy, so I was assigned to cover his position. I wasn't as familiar with the Sisters and Redmond districts as he, but I figured that with the assistance of my maps and directions from dispatchers, I would be able to find my way around. I ran from call to call, and around ten o'clock, I dealt with a domestic, hoping things would soon calm down. After leaving the jail around midnight, I received a call from a woman in Terrebonne who had been awakened by intruders in her home. The caller reported that she had seen lights on the fleeing vehicle, so she believed the suspects had a full-sized pickup with clearance lights over the canopy.

The living room and dining room of her house had been ransacked, and it was hard for me to understand how the thieves could be so brazen as to take as much time as they did inside, all the while a single mother and her teenage daughter were just down the hall. I took a list of the items that the woman knew were missing and told her to call us with a full list. I also went to the driveway, where I noticed tire tracks from dual rear tires. I provided this information to dispatch, and an ATL was put out.

No more than one hundred yards north of the ransacked home, I located a car with its gas cap off, glove box open, and items strewn about inside. I provided the license plate number to dispatch and learned that it had been stolen out of Redmond earlier in the shift. Dispatch sent out a tow truck, and around two o'clock, I was cleared to start searching for the burglars' pickup. The next dispatch call I received was a request for me to call my victim back. When I did, she told me her motor home was missing. She said that she now believed the clearance lights she saw were actually the cab-over lights on her motor home. She also told me that she believed the motor home's fuel tank was close to empty.

I chose to drive all of the back roads in the area, thinking I may find the motor home abandoned like the stolen car from Redmond. I didn't know the roads I was traveling on well, but I figured that by reading the street signs and using my map, I could at least do an adequate job of searching the area.

I turned onto one road, unable to locate a street sign, and just as I approached a small hill, I saw clearance lights approaching. Sure enough, this was a smaller motor home matching the description of my stolen vehicle. I turned to follow it but was hesitant to tell dispatch of my activity because I couldn't provide them with my location. I followed the motor home until I passed a visible street sign, and by that time I had also gotten close enough to provide dispatch with the license number. I waited for what seemed like an eternity, but was probably less than a minute, for dispatch to respond. I spoke up and asked them if the license number I gave them matched the stolen motor home. I was advised to stand by. I then heard the sergeant ask dispatch if I was behind the stolen motor home. The dispatcher confirmed that I was and again went silent. The sergeant sounded a little upset and directed dispatch to get cover units heading my way.

I continued to follow the motor home, and each time I passed a street sign, I provided dispatch with my location. I didn't want to initiate a high-risk traffic stop until I had at least one cover officer. I realized that I ultimately didn't have a choice, as the motor home turned onto a private drive. I provided dispatch the address, which I read from the fire marker, and told them I would be initiating a stop there.

I turned on my overhead lights and started to think about where I would position myself once the vehicles stopped. On an extremely dark night, we were in an area of juniper trees with homes resting on parcels of about twenty acres each. As I pulled down the lane, I saw a rock wall about three feet high off to my right. As soon as the motor home stopped, I exited my patrol car, locked the doors, ran around to the rear, jumped over the rock wall, and ran up to the front passenger's side of the motor home. Behind the cover of the rock wall, I called out to the motor home's occupants and ordered them to exit from the passenger's side. A woman exited from the front passenger's seat, and following my directions, she left the door open, allowing me to see the driver. He reached for something under the seat, and as I yelled at the passenger to get down on the ground, the driver rolled out of the driver's side.

I shifted focus from the passenger to the motor home to the front driver's side and then to the back of the motor home, wondering where the driver was, whether anyone else was in the vehicle ready to jump out, and what the driver grabbed from under the seat. I had my gun out and I shouted for the passenger to get to the ground. She refused and then said, "Fuck you!" and started to walk away from me. I was in full panic mode, but because I could see the passenger didn't have a gun, I was more worried about where the driver was. I spotted him when he peeked around the front of the motor home. I then saw his right hand reach into his coat near his waist. Instantly I thought he had a gun. I knew my situation was bad and believed I was in for a shoot out. I reverted to similar scenarios I had seen in training. What stuck in my mind was that action is quicker than reaction. Even with my gun drawn, a suspect could act by drawing and firing his gun before I could react by pulling the trigger. I took aim and started to squeeze the trigger, yelling, "Drop it! Drop it now!" I then saw an item fall to the ground and his hand open up. I eased the tension in my trigger finger and watched as he took off running away from me.

I don't know why but I decided to pursue the driver on foot. I hadn't checked the motor home for additional suspects, and I could no longer see where the passenger was, but my irrational instinct was to run directly in front of the motor home after the man. I got to within an arm's reach of him but lost grip of his overcoat. I was right on his heels when he hopped over a fence. I followed him over the fence and used the hand carrying my flashlight to brace myself. During the descent, I lost the grip on my flashlight.

By the time I recovered it, I had lost sight of the suspect. I stopped and listened for sounds of movement, but I had a hard time hearing anything except the dull thumps of my own heartbeat deep within my ears. Panic again set in, and I realized that my situation couldn't get much worse. I hunkered down and radioed dispatch to ask where my cover units were. The dispatcher responded by asking what the address was at my location. I couldn't believe she had not written down what I had read off the fire marker. I explained I didn't have the address but that I had called it out when I was pulling down the driveway. I told her to have the officers respond to my area and look for my emergency lights, which were still on.

I waited for a few more minutes, and since I could not hear or see any activity, I decided to walk back to the motor home. When I arrived, I located a portable police scanner lying where the suspect had finally complied with my command to drop it. I did a quick check to make sure no one else was in the motor home and waited for my backup.

It was starting to get light and our efforts to locate the suspects were going unrewarded. Around seven in the morning, we called off our search, and I was able to return to the office to complete my reports. I gave good descriptions of the suspects, but we had no idea who they were.

Once in bed, I found myself reliving this event. Uninterrupted sleep became next to impossible. Just as I had after previous traumatic events, I repeatedly went through this scenario, and each time, the nightmare had a different devastating ending. In one ending I shot an unarmed man. In the next I waited a split second too long to pull the trigger and I was shot. In still another I ran into additional assailants as I ran wildly in front of the unsecured motor home.

About two weeks later, I was in talking with the detective sergeant. I saw several pictures on his desk and immediately recognized one of them as the woman from the motor home. He said that he wanted to get a photo lineup of her possible associates, and when he did, I immediately picked out the driver. The detectives obtained a search warrant and asked if I wanted to tag along.

The detectives were in charge of the case, and my job was to provide uniformed security and transport. They completed the search and turned the suspect over to me for transport. As soon as I saw him, I reacted to some of my built-up frustration and let him know what he had put me through. I told him that he had almost gotten himself shot and that his behavior should have gotten him shot. I told him that I kept reliving the situation and that it was making my life miserable. I explained that in my mind, I kept coming back to a fatal conclusion, with either me being killed or me killing an unarmed person. I ended the lecture by saying that he had placed both of us in danger and that in the future he had to obey police commands or be willing to face the consequences.

He was quiet for a few minutes, and then he said, "I'm sorry." He added that he had been on a meth binge and hadn't been thinking clearly. He said he would cooperate and take me to another stolen vehicle. I pulled off the road and called for the detective sergeant. When he arrived, I told him of the suspect's admissions, and he told me that the suspect had earlier invoked his right to silence. I told the sergeant that I hadn't been questioning but rather lecturing the suspect and that he had chosen to tell me he wanted to cooperate. We then recovered a stolen pickup, and I completed my transport.

The woman pleaded guilty, but the man chose to fight the charges. Of course, the defense went through a motion to suppress, and the judge ruled in his favor, saying that although I had not questioned the defendant, I had spoken to him before he was allowed an opportunity to speak with counsel; therefore, his admission would not be allowed as evidence.

The case went to trial, and several days into the process, I was asked about the car found near the victim's home. I responded that it had been stolen from a Redmond home. The defense team objected and demanded a mistrial. The judge agreed that I had brought another stolen-vehicle crime into this case that had never been attributed to the defendant, and therefore, it would unfairly prejudice the jury. I felt awful; I could not believe that I was now the cause of a mistrial. The district attorney handling the case was extremely upset but committed to starting the trial over immediately. We ultimately won a conviction; however, my negative opinion of defense attorneys was strengthened when this attorney chose, as his only tactic, to discredit me and my observation skills. It seemed as if I were on trial, not the defendant. This further reinforced my preference for obtaining confessions and keeping victims from having to testify.

. . .

On a day shift around noon, I was given a sexual-assault case. A four-year-old boy was brought to the sheriff's office by his grandmother, who had been providing the child's day care. She was furious as she told me that her grandson had told her that a neighbor man had touched his penis. I was allowed to speak with the child alone, and for a four-year-old, he gave me a pretty clear description of a man performing oral sex on him. He said he had gone into this man's trailer after they fished in the nearby pond. The boy also described lotion and candles inside the trailer.

I spoke once again with the grandmother, and she confirmed that the boy had been allowed to visit the neighbor and that they did pretend to fish in the nearby pond. I asked that she take the boy home, explaining that I would come by later to talk with her and the boy's parents.

I gathered as much information about the suspect as I could. He had no prior sexual-assault charges, and it appeared his only source of income was a job as a bulk paper-delivery person. I went to his property, where a house was under construction, and found him living in a small camper trailer. He said he had no idea why I was there, but he agreed to talk with me. He confirmed that the boy was over earlier that day but insisted nothing had happened. He allowed me to take a look inside his trailer, and just as the boy had described, there was a bottle of lotion and candles on the table. I talked with the suspect a while longer and felt that he was too comfortable at home, so at this time, about five thirty, I asked him to come with me to the sheriff's office. He agreed, and we walked toward my patrol car.

The boy's father arrived at the grandmother's home, and it was obvious that he had been told about the abuse. He had a determined look as he strode quickly in our direction, screaming at the suspect. I don't recall exactly what he said, but all I could think was that I had to get the father back in the house. I yelled, "Not now. Turn around and go back in the house, and I will talk with you later." To my surprise, he turned and, just as quickly as he approached, retreated inside.

I had a sick feeling that the father retreated too quickly and easily, and I became concerned that he may have returned to the house for a firearm. I told the suspect to hurry up, and we quickstepped to my patrol car. Oddly, I wanted to create some distance between him and me thinking that if the dad did open fire, I didn't want to be hit accidently. Luckily that didn't happen, and we got to the car and left.

Once we were at the sheriff's office, I took the suspect into a four-by-five foot interview room. We talked for nearly an hour, and I used the time to gather information about his childhood and drug use. I got to the point where I was confident that he had molested the child, and I then transitioned into an interrogation. I hit him with themes about his being the victim of abuse as a child and the possibility that drugs had influenced him to do something he wouldn't normally do. The suspect sat quietly and didn't react to my accusations. His silence only reinforced my belief that he was guilty. I kept repeating the themes, and finally he lowered his head and raised his hands to his eyes as if he were becoming emotional. I moved closer to him and asked him if this was the first time he had done something like this, and he said it was. I then wanted to lock him into his confession, so I asked him how it got to that point. I naturally thought he would jump on one of my previous themes about his being a victim or losing control under the influence of drugs. To my surprise, he said, "I wanted to teach the boy a lesson." I asked him to tell me what the boy had done. He said, "He has been a flirt, and I wanted to teach him what could happen if he continues to flirt."

I had taught myself not to react in situations like this, but I couldn't help thinking of my four-year-old son at home and how innocent he or any four-year-old was. The thought of this man doing those things to the small boy made me nauseous. I had my probable cause and knew his confession was damning, so I arrested him for first-degree sodomy and immediately transferred him to the book-in counter. It was generally the responsibility of the arresting officer to complete all of the booking paperwork; however, I explained that I was not feeling well and asked that the corrections staff take over my duties. They agreed, and I told them I would be next door in case they needed anything else.

I needed some time to let this settle before I could start my report. I was sitting quietly in the office when the phone rang. It was a member of the corrections staff; the suspect had asked to use the bathroom, and while in there, he had tried to flush his bra and panties down the toilet. The staff member said that not only had he been wearing female undergarments but also that his entire body, including his chest and pubic area, was shaved. After a few minutes, I went to the grandmother's home to thank the father for following my instructions and to tell the entire family that the suspect had confessed and was now locked up in jail. I wasn't surprised to learn that the suspect, wanting nothing to do with a courtroom, had pleaded guilty.

.   .   .

It was early afternoon New Years Day 1994 and our shift had been quiet. I met up with the sergeant and another deputy at the county fuel pumps and we spent a few minutes talking about how few calls there had been. I was the first to leave and traveled north on 27th Street until the first stop light at Highway 20. Two cars were directly in front of me traveling in the same direction. We had a green light and I watched as the front vehicle slammed on its brakes, causing the second vehicle to run into the lead car. I turned on my emergency lights and was in the process of calling in the accident when I saw the driver of the front car, a male—standing about six feet four inches and weighing two hundred forty pounds—walk right up to the driver's window of the second vehicle and he punched through the window, shattering the glass and striking the driver who was still seated in his car.

I called in an assault in progress and requested back-up. I started shouting commands at the large assailant, already concerned about how I would handle it if he chose not to obey, but I was able to get him to move to the front of his car. I was about even with the second car when this driver stepped out. He was a Samoan who was about six feet three inches and two hundred seventy-five pounds. He was clinching his fists, staring directly at the assailant and I knew he was ready to fight.

I stepped in front of the Samoan and told him to move to the back of his car. The first driver was now shouting at the Samoan and yelling something about following too close. The Samoan had his small child with him and told me he would lose face, in front of his boy, if he didn't fight back. He started past me and I grabbed his bicep, with both hands, and it was then, feeling like I was in trouble, that I realized I had another deputy and a city officer now fighting with the assailant.

I kept talking, begging, the Samoan not to make matters worse and for some reason I was able to get him to listen. The other officers, uniforms torn and disheveled, were now in the ditch but had the assailant under control. I approached the female passenger, of the first vehicle, and she said that her husband had "anger control issues" and he had slammed on his brakes when he thought the car behind him was following too close.

Both the sergeant and other deputy blamed me, for the entire altercation, because I had talked about it being quiet. Years later the sheriff's office would be called to a shooting in the Tumalo area. The female victim had been involved in a domestic with her husband and when she was running away he started shooting a rifle at her. It turned out that this was the same couple that had been in that first car. It appeared that her husband still had "anger control issues" and she was lucky to be alive. The husband eventually was convicted of attempted murder and sent to the pen.

.   .   .

It was a night shift and around midnight when I was dispatched to a rural residence east of Bend for an unknown disturbance. The home owner was awakened to shouts being heard coming from his private drive. This area was one of the primary routes between Bend and Prineville and an area of small, twenty acre, ranches. I arrived at the address and found a vehicle parked just off the road at the private drive. I started walking towards the home and came across three men who were walking back towards their car and me. They told me that their friend was drunk and wanted to fight. After spending the night drinking they were on their way back home to Prineville when their buddy demanded that they stop the car. They said he was not making any sense and began walking towards the residence. They tried to restrain him and get him back in the car but they could not do it.

I walked about two hundred feet further and met the intoxicated six feet five inch cowboy who wanted to fight. I tried to convince him that he needed to listen to his friends and let them take him home where he could sleep it off but he reacted by saying "Who's going to make me." I tried again to convince him to listen to his friends but by now he was totally focused on me. He had assumed a boxer's stance, bladed body with his fists up, and began challenging me by saying, "Come on, let's go." I pulled the capstun from its holder and pointing it in his direction I said "Stop, don't do it or I will spray you!" I continued to yell at him to stop and he continued at me now cocking his right fist back when I sent the pepper spray into his face and at the same time I pivoted away from the direction of his attack. I yelled continually, "go to the ground" "all the way down" even after he went to one knee. He was moaning loudly and using his hands to try and wipe away the irritant. I was content on waiting until he completely submitted before even attempting to place him in handcuffs. Just then a small female deputy arrived and did a body slam into his back, knocking him to the ground. She then began to try and control his arms and by this time I had put my capstun away and joined in the fray.

We soon had him in cuffs and in the back of her patrol car. I asked why she had been so quick to go hands on with the much bigger suspect and she said that when she arrived she could hear our shouts and the three friends, knowing what their buddy was like, told her, "Your partner is in trouble!" She saw him on his knees and not sure if I was hurt, she just reacted. It was nice to know that she would be there to help, regardless the size of the threat.

Chapter Seven

Deschutes County Investigations

In September 1994, I accepted a transfer into investigations. The sergeant's philosophy was that each detective should be able to handle any case, and therefore he distributed all cases to us equally. It wasn't unusual that some officers shied away from child abuse or sex crimes. None of them would intentionally hurt an investigation, but some were not very skilled in communicating with children or young girls and therefore may not have gathered enough credible information to proceed. I volunteered to take the bulk of the sex crimes, and although I didn't formally change the sergeant's protocol, I would informally take other sex-crimes when detectives asked.

One such case was of the long-term molestation of a five-year-old girl and an eight-year-old boy. Because of the extent of the abuse, the interviews were draining and took the better part of a day. Both children were able to provide information that was later verified and that added to their credibility. My initial search for the suspect found that he had moved to the Oregon coast, and because of the extent of the crimes, I asked permission to travel there to conduct my own interview. I was told that because of financial constraints, I would not be allowed to travel; however, I was put in contact with the state police and assured that they would do a good job with the interview.

I didn't believe I was the only person who could get a confession, but I couldn't help but think that transferring the case to someone else, who had not spent hours interviewing the children as I had, could result in an interview that would be less effective than one I would have conducted. I anxiously waited for the call from the investigator. When it came, the investigator started by saying, "Good news. I got a full confession." I felt relieved, but out of habit, I responded, "You're kidding." He then said, "Yes, I am." He hadn't gotten to talk with the suspect because the suspect had been arrested on a parole violation and was in the process of being shipped back to Deschutes County.

I checked with parole and probation and confirmed that he had been arrested and was in transit. I contacted the jail to check his planned time of arrival. I and another detective were there waiting for the suspect upon his arrival. I would conduct the interview, and the second detective would watch from an adjacent room and run the recording equipment.

I first informed the suspect that our conversation would be recorded and advised him of his rights. I asked him questions about who he was and about his life, hoping that he would forget about the recording. It wasn't long before he admitted to drug use and coming from an abusive home. I next focused on what he thought about the children I had interviewed, and he assured me that they were great kids and that he loved them. I took advantage of this and threw out reasons why I thought he had done these things to the children. I brought up his own upbringing and suggested that this physical contact, although abusive, was still a method he used to reach out and show affection. I also brought up how drugs make people do things that they wouldn't normally do and how I often came across people who were sorry for what they had done. I pointed out how respectable it was for people to stand up and admit their mistakes. I could see that my approach was getting to him, as he had buried his face in his hands and started to cry, so I leaned closer to him and quietly said, "You are sorry about what has taken place, aren't you?" He said he was, and then he repeated that he loved the children and that they were good kids. He said they were telling the truth about everything. I sat in the room as he quietly recounted each of the incidents, validating each of the children's claims.

Once the man had been booked for the new charges, I spoke with the other detective. He said he had never seen anything quite like my interview, especially my ability to break him down so quickly. During the course of my interview I had asked if any of this man's activities had occurred outside our county, and he said that he may have been involved in unacceptable behavior with a girl on the coast. I decided to call the state trooper back. "How did it go?" he asked. I said, "Great. I got a full confession." He then said sarcastically that he wouldn't fall for that, but I said, "No, I got a full confession and an admission that he may have been involved with a girl in your jurisdiction." The trooper realized that I was telling the truth and gave me a legitimate, "Great job!" No evidence of crimes could be found on the coast, but the suspect pleaded guilty to our charges and received an extensive sentence.

. . .

I had started to build a reputation for suspect interviews and soon was being used solely for suspect contact. Other detectives would take the initial case, work it through, and provide me with the details, and then I would complete the interview. A detective had been working one such case, in which two teenage girls reported long-term abuse and rape by their biological grandfather. The girls had basically been abandoned by their mother, so the grandparents were now their guardians.

The other detective and I decided that we would contact the grandparents at home. I would ask the grandfather to come with me to the sheriff's office while she would then interview the grandmother at the home. I introduced myself to the grandfather and explained that we had some concerns about the girls and asked for his help in our investigation. He said that he had just gotten home from work, so I asked him what he did. He told me that he was a drywaller, and I told him how hard I thought that job was and that I was amazed how he was able to handle such a job at his age. These pleasantries seemed to gain his trust, and he agreed to go with me to the sheriff's office.

One freedom we police used to have was that we were not required to record all suspect interviews. (Because police tactics are constantly being scrutinized, this tactic is now under fire.) If I thought a suspect may have been too concerned about the tape recorder to open up, as happened in a lot of cases, I would proceed without a recorder. However, I would bring in a second officer to validate the admissions or turn on the recorder after the ice had been broken and the confession made to validate the confession. I always clearly documented the entire interview and confession in my report.

On this occasion, I was able to get a full confession from the grandfather, and along with his confession came his desire to tell the girls that he was sorry. I used this as an opportunity to bring in the lead detective. I told the grandfather that she had been working with the girls and that he could tell her what he wanted to pass on to them. She came in, and with some prodding, he repeated the same statement of his acts of rape and abuse.

His defense attorney's strategy was also to file a motion to suppress. He tried to get the suspect's statements thrown out by attacking me and my "questionable" police tactics. I was accused of being too nice and of tricking an uneducated man. He argued that the written confession could not have been made by this illiterate man. In presenting our case, the district attorney showed that the only written product was the man's signature on the advice-of-rights card. Although the statement had not been recorded, the judge found that it was made voluntarily and validated by the lead officer. This case also ended in a guilty plea and a long prison sentence.

. . .

Interviewing suspects of sex crimes or child abuse wasn't easy. I paid an emotional price for always trying to show empathy with those who committed these hideous acts. I also paid when I wasn't successful in gaining a confession. On several occasions I would conduct the initial investigation and then attempt an interview with the suspect only to be met with a reluctance to admit any wrongdoing or, more often, with an invocation of the right to remain silent. Over the years a handful of these suspects chose to take their own lives after my initial interview. Police officers' weird sense of humor explained why other officers might call me Dr. Death or give me credit for truly rehabilitating the suspect, but regardless of what they said, these suicides bothered me. I would have thoughts about me being the last person to speak with the suspect, and I also felt my actions may have pushed them into it. I went through a period of self-criticism, thinking I should have known they would try this and that I should have done something to prevent it.

Chapter Eight

A Friend's Betrayal

Each detective was responsible for taking on active investigations that other detectives were unable to finish. One such case was a missing-person report that came to our sheriff's office in December of 1992. The report listed Steven Novakowski as missing and last seen in the Redmond area in July of that year. This case was transferred to a new detective, and she wasted no time in getting me interested in the report.

When Steven Novakowski was about fifteen years old, he became friends with Travis Peterson and soon found himself living with Travis and Travis's uncle and aunt, Ron and Roberta. It appeared that during this period, Steven began and ended a relationship with a girlfriend, and ultimately the girlfriend became Travis's wife. Ron's entire family was fascinated by Steven in a way that had previously been reserved for Travis.

Steven's biological family had concerns about his relationship with Travis, Ron, and Roberta, so during his junior year, his parents sent Steven to live with his uncle in Laughlin, Nevada. Steven returned to live with his parents in Bullhead City, Arizona, for his senior year. In 1989, he enlisted in the navy, and he served two tours of duty on the USS *Elliott* during Desert Storm. According to his father, Steven had plans to return to Nevada and start his own business, but his family last heard from him in July, shortly after he had been discharged. Steven's family believed that, at that time, Steven was staying in Redmond with Ron and Roberta as part of "the family."

In December of 1992, Steven's grandmother from Pennsylvania made the initial missing-person report, and she regularly called for updates and pushed to make sure this case did not go cold. She reported that she knew something was wrong on her birthday, July 26, 1992. She said, until then, Steven had never missed calling her on her birthday.

Ron, Roberta, and the entire family had been interviewed. The reports indicated that on Sunday, July 19, the family came together for a barbecue. Steven was seen walking away from the home, possibly to get cigarettes, but he never returned.

One disconcerting confidential statement came from someone who had been close to a member of the Redmond family. Because of justified concerns for personal safety, the informant made it clear that they did not want their name listed in any report and said that they would never be willing to testify to what they were telling detectives. This statement, although complete hearsay, summarized that Travis and Steven had gone out onto public land and that only Travis returned. He returned with a large black garbage bag and made a joke about shaking hands with Steven for the last time. He proceeded to open the bag as if to indicate Steven's hands were inside.

The other detective and I started spending all our spare time learning everything we could about the family, Steven, and Travis. We also began the task of learning how to conduct a no-body homicide investigation. One of the biggest hurdles would be proving that Steven was dead, and this could only be done through due diligence—by checking every possible hospital, police agency and multiple credit agencies, banks, and government agencies to show there had not been any contact with Steven Novakowski. We also decided that, generally on Friday's, when we were not busy; we should spend some time on our public lands in hopes of finding bones or a potential grave site.

The background information gave us the profile of Travis as being a self-proclaimed ninja, practicing martial arts and never being far from a knife. According to former friends, he had a fascination with death and talked like he could kill. At one time, while living in

Arizona, he was seen with a homemade garrote. A former girlfriend also told us that Travis had once hid in the bushes and caught her kissing another man. Travis became irate and ordered her into the home, and he and the other man left. Travis later returned and told her that he had choked the man with his garrote but had not killed him. She said that he then pulled a knife on her and cut a notch of skin just above her breast, saying he was making his mark. She also said that a few days later, she saw the other man and noticed that he had a red mark around his neck.

Detectives in Arizona tracked down this other man, and he confirmed that Travis had attacked him. He told detectives that Travis thought of himself as a ninja and had a uniform and all different types of weapons that he carried on him. When asked about the attack, the man described how Travis confronted him over his relationship with the girlfriend and then took him out to an isolated location. When the man started to walk away, Travis attacked him from behind with the garrote. He explained that Travis did let him go but that the mark stayed on his neck for about three weeks. He told the detectives that Travis was only dealing with reality 20 percent of the time and in that other 80 percent of the time, in his fantasy life, he was capable of killing someone.

Ron and Roberta were currently living in a small home on about seven acres adjacent to Highway 97 and the railroad tracks almost halfway between Redmond and Bend. Their home was across the road from several thousand acres of public land. Ron, a borderline alcoholic, would periodically work at low-income jobs and appeared to have some income from workers' compensation injury claims. Roberta worked at a local grocery store, and the family did not have many outside friends or associates.

Drafting an affidavit became one of my responsibilities. Although the other detective and I documented everything we learned in police reports, we also wanted to transfer the information to an affidavit so that when we believed we had enough for a search warrant, we would be ready to go.

The other detective believed that we needed to interview each member of the family again, in hopes that we would gather new information or at least get statements that we could eventually prove false. The concern with this approach was that the family had very little tying them to our community, so if we applied too much pressure, they would move. This would then make our seemingly impossible task even more difficult. We took on the Columbo approach. Anyone who has watched *Columbo* knows that the detective came across as not very bright. He would ask inconspicuous questions and the suspects, not feeling threatened, answered, locking them into incriminating statements.

We started with immediate family members and wanted to keep the questions nonthreatening. We asked questions like, Who was there? What did they eat? Where did they think Steven had gone? What were the attitudes and emotions of people on the day Steven left? It was amazing that the family hadn't rehearsed answers to simple questions like these. We got answers about who was present at the barbecue that ranged from just family and Steven to family, grandmother, Steven, Travis, and Travis's girlfriend, Shawna, to even more extensive gatherings of family, grandmother, Steven, Travis, Travis's girlfriend, and Travis's brother and his family. As for what they ate, we heard the typical hot dogs and hamburgers, we heard chicken, and Ron said he recalled making the favorite family recipe of barbecue corned beef. When it came to where Steven went, they started by saying they had no idea and thought he was just going for a walk toward Redmond to the closest store, about a mile away, for cigarettes. Ron stated that Steven had talked about Thailand and a girl he met there while he was in the navy. Other family members said that Steven had been depressed and had often talked about the trains that went by the house and wondered where they went, leading them to think he had jumped a train. They weren't even consistent about when he left, some saying he walked away prior to lunch, others saying he went for a walk after everyone ate. As far as emotions, some people told us it was a pleasant day and everyone was happy, others said that only Steven seemed upset, and still others made statements that Travis and Ron were upset and that Steven was quiet.

I clearly recall our first interview with Ron and how nervous I was. I knew Steven was dead and that Ron at least knew about it. I didn't want to blow the investigation by putting too much pressure on him, but at the same time, I wanted to get him locked in to several key statements. We decided to use a larger conference room and to sit across from Ron at a table. (This arrangement, we reasoned, would be a more relaxed and less threatening than a traditional four-by-five-foot interview room with only two chairs stationed in close proximity.) During my interview, I realized that my leg was involuntarily bouncing up and down. I was glad we had the table to hide this, but I found it amazing what nerves will do. I really tried to focus on calming myself down, but I continually licked my lips to keep my mouth from drying up, all the while trying not to come across as nervous. Ultimately, I think the only reason Ron didn't notice my nerves was because he, with just cause, was more nervous than I. He was extremely talkative and took very little prodding to tell us about his relationship with Steven. Ron said that he had helped Steven get a job but that Steven had walked off the job, causing the employer to become upset with Ron. Ron said that this had upset him and that he then had some words with Steven about this on Saturday, but on Sunday, the day Steven walked away, everything was good.

On April 5, 1995, the other detective and I went to Travis's home in Tumalo, Oregon, to talk with Travis and his girlfriend, Shawna. Travis said that on the day of the barbecue, Ron had been told about Steven sleeping with a relative of Ron's and that Ron was upset and had confronted Steven about it. During the confrontation, Roberta stuck up for Steven, and Travis said that family members then wondered whether Roberta was also sleeping with Steven. Travis said that the next thing he knew, Steven walked away and did not return.

I spoke with Shawna alone, and she too talked about Ron being upset about the news of Steven sleeping with a relative. She recalled that Travis's brother and family were at the barbecue, and when I first asked if she had spoken with Steven, she said she had not. I explained that I had heard that Steven, Travis, and she had gone for a walk together. She then confirmed that they did go for a short walk down the canal and that Travis and Steven talked about old times in Arizona. After they returned, Steven walked off alone.

During our visit, I saw a sword lying in the living room along with what appeared to be the head of a hatchet. The other detective also said that she saw several bladed weapons in the home.

During one of the other detective's visits to Ron and Roberta's new residence, Roberta showed her the family portrait. It showed Roberta and the children with Steven standing behind Roberta with his hand on her shoulder. Only Ron was missing from this large family portrait. During this visit, the other detective asked for Steven's writings, and Roberta turned over notebooks containing the writings and some pictures. The other detective then arranged for a psychic to meet with us. She had heard that psychics had been useful in other major investigations, and after this psychic contacted her asking if she could help, the detective set up the meeting.

I am not the type to ever initiate a psychic in an investigation, but I thought it might be fun to go along for the ride. This psychic used Steven's notebook to get close to him. After spending time with her eyes closed and hand on the notebook, she frowned and winced as if she were involved in a struggle. She was visibly upset and started talking about an evil person. She told us that Steven was dead, that he had been killed by an evil man who had killed before, or will kill again, maybe even while in prison. She then spent some time trying to understand where Steven's remains were. She got a vision of water, but then she had a vision of him being spread out over a large area. She could not be any more specific on the location.

On June 29, 1995, the other detective and I went to Salem to talk with Travis's brother. He told us that he had gone by Ron and Roberta's on the weekend that Steven left and was in the process of moving from Redmond to La Pine. He stopped by for a few minutes before going back to Redmond to clean up their old home. He said that he recalled some conversation about Steven sleeping with a family member and that Travis was talking like they needed to do something to Steven. He went on to say that he already knew Travis did not like

Steven and that this dislike originated when they were both living in Arizona. The brother said he got the feeling that he was being drawn into a plan to go with Travis to beat Steven up. He said he had made it clear that he wanted no part in that and left. He assured us that he did not know anything else.

During our search of financial records, we found three checks, written by Ron and Roberta, and issued to Travis's brother totaling $530, between July 21, 1992, and August 18, 1992. This caused us additional concern about his possible involvement, so we went back to Salem on July 12, 1995. He told us that he could not think of any reason why he had been given those checks but said he would help us if he could. We used this offer to gain his cooperation in making a phone call to Roberta. He said he did not have her number, but he agreed to call his grandmother in Arizona, who would know it.

We recorded the phone conversation between him and his grandmother. He explained that he needed Ron and Roberta's phone number because he wanted to talk to them about police trying to locate him. His grandmother then offered that the police were looking for him to ask questions about Steven. She added that the story she told police was about the barbecue. He said, "I don't remember any barbecue," and she responded, "There wasn't a barbecue."

He reluctantly dialed the phone number his grandmother provided to speak to Roberta; however, Ron answered. The other detective and I could only hear his side of the conversation. He explained his concern that the police were looking for him. There was a pause, and then he said, "Yes." After getting off the phone, he told us that Ron had said that the police were just trying to figure out what happened to Steven and that the family members were all telling the police that Steven walked away before dinner. He also said that the police had asked questions about relationships between Steven and family members and that Ron did not think the police needed to know any of that information.

We left, but before we headed back over the Cascade Mountains, we stopped for lunch and listened to the taped conversation between

Ron and Travis's brother. During the conversation, Ron said, "You know, it's about the stupid stunt your brother pulled." That was when Travis's brother responded, "Yes." This told us that we were still not getting the entire truth from him, so we returned and confronted him one more time. This time he said that Travis had been saying he wanted to kill Steven, and that was what had gotten Ron worked up. He said that he had heard Ron give them permission to "take care of it." It was then Travis's brother realized that Travis was trying to get him to help kill Steven. He said he was present when Travis and Shawna went off with Steven, but he insisted that he had nothing to do with what happened next. He and his wife then left without finding out what actually happened to Steven.

We were now getting close to the completion of our affidavit. We submitted the rough draft to the district attorney's office, and after a few revisions, we submitted it to a circuit court judge for review. After a few more revisions, we began the buildup to a search with officers from Bend, Redmond, the Oregon State Police, the Oregon Department of Justice, members of Department of Human Services (DHS looking into ongoing concerns for child neglect) and the Oregon National Guard. Our plan was to have three search teams and teams of two investigators conduct eleven different interviews.

I spent so much time at home in quiet thought about the case, trying to go through all scenarios, hoping we weren't missing anything. I was regularly getting headaches too, and the doctor told me they were probably stress related. A good friend approached me and asked what was bothering me. I told him that I couldn't share the details but explained there was a lot going on at work. My wife and I sent our children to stay with my parents since I knew the next week would be crazy.

As the other detective and I were trying to gather as much information as possible about our suspects, we both spent our off-duty hours conducting surveillance. We wanted to make sure that we knew where all of our key players would be when we initiated the searches, and we wanted to catch them alone and away from any weapons. Our search was set for Monday, July 31, 1995, at seven thirty in the morning, but we decided to approach and interview one family member on Sunday night in hopes of strengthening our case prior to the key interviews with Travis, Ron, and Roberta.

We picked up that family member and her spouse and took them to the sheriff's office, where we had staged a room with charts and filing cabinets all labeled "Novakowski Homicide." There, we conducted a tape-recorded interview. We explained that we were part of a task force now investigating the homicide of Steven Novakowski. She replied, "Do you really know he's dead, or do you just think you know?" The other detective assured her that we knew, and the family member then explained that Steven was having a relationship with a family member and that Travis told Ron about it. Ron became upset, and she watched as Travis and Shawna went for a walk with Steven. When Travis and Shawna returned, she said, they had only a black garbage bag with them, and Travis bragged about it containing Steven's head and hands. He opened the bag so the other family members could confirm he was telling the truth.

We typed up the interview and had it ready for our 5:00 a.m. briefing. The family member and spouse spent the night in a guarded motel room, and we made sure they had no phones. We thought this give us the best chance of success for our three-team search the next morning. I gave out assignments, and when I spoke about taking Travis down by means of a traffic stop, just after leaving his home on his way work, the district attorney spoke up, saying he did not want any arrests made before the DA's office gave approval.

We, the detectives, had previously gone over our options and believed that we had probable cause for an arrest. We also believed that an arrest would confirm to the suspects that we had evidence and therefore would be more conducive to successful interviews. I spoke up for our plan, saying that we had the authority to arrest on probable cause. The DA looked at me like I had no idea what I was doing. Just then, the detective sergeant stepped up and told the DA that we had a plan to gain all of the suspects' cooperation in interviews but to make arrests if we had to. The sergeant then asked that the DA speak alone with him out of the briefing area. They then left, and we continued our briefing.

I soon was staged outside Ron and Roberta's apartment, waiting for word that Travis was on the move. Once that traffic stop was initiated, we would move in on our targets. Mine being to contact Ron and ask that he go with me to the sheriff's office. This waiting was more stressful than any anxiety I had experienced before. I reassured myself that just like in any high school sporting event, all of the nerves would subside as soon as the ball was put in play. The traffic stop was made, and I and a detective sergeant moved in on Ron. We gained his cooperation, and he voluntarily went with us to our interview location.

Ron initially denied that he knew what happened to Steven and insisted that he had been busy cooking his corned beef on the barbecue. Approximately thirty minutes later, Ron was defeated, and he admitted his part in Steven's demise. His statement was that Travis had told him that Steven was having sex with a female family member, which got Ron upset with Steven. Travis then told Ron that Steven needed to be taken care of, and after several minutes of prodding, Ron told Travis, "Take care of it."

Ron said that he did not want to believe Steven was dead. He had hoped that Travis had just knocked him around and that Steven had just walked off. Travis did return with a black garbage bag, however, and he told Ron that it contained Steven's head and hands. Ron told us that he then drove Travis and his brother out to China Hat Road, where Travis then walked over a hill out of Ron's view. He returned a short time later without the bag. It appeared that Travis's brother still had not been completely honest with us and would need and additional interview.

Ron agreed to take us out to China Hat Road where Travis had disposed of the black bag. Before ending the interview, I asked Ron to tell me what he had been thinking during our first interview. He said that he was freaking out and acknowledged that it wouldn't have taken much more pressure from me for him to have confessed. As we finalized the plan for our trip to China Hat Road, I called the other detective. She told me that Travis had also confessed. We had spent a great deal of time and anxiety planning just how we wanted this investigation to end, and it appeared that all of our planning was now paying off. We gave each other a few minutes of praise, but then we realized that this wasn't just a story being told around a campfire; it was real, and a young man's life had been taken away.

Ron took us out and directed us to the general area where he had turned off the road and last seen Travis. Travis was now on his way out to show the other detective where the remains were, so we went back to the office and booked Ron on murder and conspiracy charges. Travis took detectives right to a lava tube, and detectives found Steven's skull and hands.

Afterward, I had a chance to talk with some of the other team leaders, and I found that most of them had never been involved in such a successful operation. The searches found notes (including a suicide pact between Travis and Shawna should they be caught), weapons (blow gun, throwing stars, sword, and Ka-Bar knives), a ninja suit, books, (*Armed and Dangerous, Mass Murderers, Serial Killers,* and *The Anarchist's Cookbook*), and Steven's belongings. All of the interview teams, with the exception of Roberta's team, had success in gathering incriminating admissions. I wasn't convinced that Roberta had no knowledge, but maybe she truly wanted to remember Steven the way she had for so long and to believe he had just walked away. Travis's and Shawna's interviews were the most informative, and they provided the following details.

When Travis told Ron about Steven's alleged relationship, Ron gave Travis permission to kill Steven, saying, "He ought to have his balls cut off." That was all Travis needed to carry out an act he had dreamed about for years. Ron may also have been concerned that Steven was sleeping with Roberta, so after getting Ron's permission, Travis asked Steven to go for a walk with him and Shawna. (We believe that the girlfriend was key to getting Steven to go with Travis, as Steven would not have thought Travis would do anything in front of her.) A lightning storm was moving in, and Travis used it as a reason for them to walk out onto public land. They would climb a small hill and watch the storm. On the hill, Travis stood behind Steven, took out his Ka-Bar knife, and knocked Steven out with the butt. While Steven was unable to defend himself, Travis tied his hands behind his back and cut his clothes off him. Then Travis cut Steven's good knee, joking that since Steven had a bad knee, Travis wanted him to be able to walk evenly in the next life. Travis bragged about making Steven play tic-tac-toe. Travis cut a board in Steven's chest and made Steven pick his choice of plays while Travis used his knife to cut the Xs and Os. Steven then made statements that got Travis even more worked up, so he cut Steven's penis off. Travis seemed pleased that he told Steven he wouldn't need it anymore and tossed it onto Steven's chest.

Steven begged Travis to finish it and put him out of his misery. About thirty minutes passed and then, at Steven's request, Travis stuck the knife into Steven's chest, finding it difficult but not impossible to get through the ribcage and into the heart. Travis knew when he had hit the heart because he could feel the heartbeat through the knife. After Steven was dead, Travis decided to cut off his head and hands, thinking this would make it impossible to identify the remains if they were found. Travis commented that cutting off a head was much more difficult than TV portrays. Then Travis and his girlfriend returned and told Ron what they had done. They agreed that Ron would take them out the following day to dispose of the head and hands. A year after the killing, Travis went back to the killing site and collected all of the other bones. He took them back to his home, where he ground them up and threw them into the nearby Deschutes River. *Maybe psychics do have something to offer*, I thought.

After giving his confession, Travis agreed to take detectives back to the killing site. In a nearby crevasse, the female detective located a large leg bone. (An examination of it found deep cuts just above the knee, confirming Travis's statement about torturing Steven.) While conducting a videotaped walk-through, we learned that the courts, without waiting for the first appearance, appointed Travis an attorney, who demanded that all contact with Travis stop.

Our interviews were now finished, and it was time to begin the reports and process the evidence. We found some humor in one of Ron's homemade videos taken outside the family's home some time after Steven had been killed, as the video showed a sheriff's office levy sign. As he focused the camera on the sign, Ron commented on how inept we were and how we should not be supported. We also talked with a female friend of Travis's, and she said that Travis could leave his body and visit her in her second-story apartment. She talked about his unusual sex drive, especially during lightening storms. I wondered, *Is each lightning storm an opportunity for him to relive his victory over Steven? Did Travis and his girlfriend have sex during the lightning storm right after Steven's demise?*

The day after the arrest the headline in our local paper read "Three Jailed in Slaying; Body Not Found." Then the following day's headline started with "Skull Unearthed in '92 Murder Probe." My neighbor friend who had previously asked if I was okay approached me and congratulated me on our success, adding he knew that I must have been behind the headlines.

We conducted one other interesting interview in Arizona with Travis's grandmother. I played her the tape in which she said there never had been a barbecue. She insisted there had been a barbecue and that that was not her voice on the tape. I told her we knew Steven was killed and that she had been lying to us. She said I was wrong. When I said that we had his head and hands and that the medical examiner had confirmed they were Steven's, she insisted that the ME was wrong and refused to change her story. We also interviewed Travis's brother again, and this time he acknowledged that he did go on the drive to China Hat and believed Travis had killed Steven, but he had been unwilling to tell us everything up front for fear of what Travis might do to him if he learned he had been talking.

Travis pleaded guilty to aggravated murder and accepted a true life sentence. Which means Travis will never be released from prison. Ron ultimately pleaded guilty to conspiracy to commit murder, and Travis's girlfriend pleaded guilty to hindering prosecution. After the sentencing, the other detective and I took Steven's grandmother to a florist and then out to the murder location. The other detective pointed out that we had been to this site during one of our Friday searches; however, we never went to the top of the hill where the murder took place and the leg was found. Steven's grandmother had a few minutes of silence and left the flowers. Before we left, she gave me a silver dollar. She said she knew it wasn't much, but she wanted me to have it as a memento of her appreciation for our effort in holding her grandson's killers accountable.

Chapter Nine

The Cases Keep Coming

Deschutes County investigations never had a shortage of work, and it seemed I was always being passed a child-abuse or sex-crime case. In one such case, a family had given a convicted sex offender a second chance and allowed him to move in with them. According to the terms of his probation, the guest was not to have any contact with children. The family believed he had been rehabilitated, and against the terms of his release, they allowed him unsupervised time with their two-year-old daughter.

After completing the typically draining interview with the two-year-old child, I contacted the suspect and had him come into the office. On this occasion, I used an interview room with a hidden camera and microphone, so I felt comfortable telling him that we were recording the interview before I advised him of his rights and moved on to basic conversation that I hoped would take his mind off the recording and allow him to speak more freely.

Just as in other interviews, I began by obtaining his history, which did contain issues with family abuse, alcohol, and limited drug use. He openly admitted to his prior abuse of children but insisted he was a changed man and would do nothing to harm his friends' child. I asked him if he could think of any innocent contact with this child that the child may have taken to be inappropriate, and he told me about an incident that happened when he was babysitting. The child wanted help getting onto a bunk bed, so, he said, he lifted the child up, placing his hand on the child's bottom.

I then talked about his history of sexual abuse and said I considered it an addiction, mentioning that he had been required to go through treatment for it. He agreed but said that he had been taught to be aware of and to avoid specific situations and activities that might tempt him to relapse. I made an analogy to an alcoholic and asked the suspect if he thought it would be good for an alcoholic to keep his refrigerator full of beer. He said no; keeping alcohol at home would cause an alcoholic to relapse.

I asked how long he had been living with the two-year-old, and he said one month. I then said that his friend had put him in a situation that was not in his best interest, and I also said the child only had spoken about one incident. I then said I doubted any alcoholic could have lasted a month in a house with alcohol before breaking down and taking a drink, so he had done a good job resisting temptation as long as he did.

By now the suspect was no longer defiant, so I kept the pressure on him by repeating the theme that he had made a single mistake, but after showing a great deal of restraint. I then asked, "It was just the one time, wasn't it?", and he said, "Yes." He elaborated that placing his hand on the two-year-old's bottom while lifting her caused him to want to touch her a little more, and he did. His statement echoed that of the child, so I was able to make the arrest. I did not believe he would want to go to trial.

I was correct: he pleaded guilty. When I spoke with his attorney, after the attorney had watched the taped interview, he said that he thought the interview was very effective, and he asked if I would be willing to talk with his children to find out what kind of mischief they have been involved in.

. . .

All detectives became involved with a case of a mother and her infant child missing from Redmond. The initial investigation provided details that her vehicle had been seen parked near the entrance to Crooked River Ranch. Some of her acquaintances told us they were concerned about her drug use and mentioned she had possibly purchased drugs in the area where she had last been seen. A sweep of the area found the car abandoned about ten miles from where it had last been seen. There was only one set of footprints around the vehicle, and they appeared to be consistent with those of the missing mother. We called out a search-and-rescue team, but its check of this immediate area came up empty.

About five days later, we received a report that the missing woman's purse had been found in an isolated area along Buckhorn Road, about ten miles from where the car had been found, and twenty from where she was last seen. Apparently the purse had actually been found the day the woman was reported missing, but the person who found it had neglected to report it until after seeing the story on the news. We sent out another search team, which discovered the bodies of the mother and child about thirty yards from the road.

The mother was wearing shorts and a sports bra, and her other clothes were later found tossed along the road. The infant lay about twenty feet from the mother, and the only injuries we found were on the infant and they appeared to be animal bite marks on its soft tissue. The medical examiner determined that the cause of death was hypothermia. The temperature had been down to about thirty-five degrees, and the ME explained that the mother's disrobing was consistent with behavior of those suffering from hypothermia. Detectives raised the question of why only the infant sustained postmortem animal bites, and we concluded that because the mother had meth in her system, an animal would have smelled the poison, which would have made her body undesirable. We later located studies that suggested an individual under the influence of meth may succumb to hypothermia quicker than someone not under its influence.

.   .   .

In the early and mid 1990s, the country saw an increase in antigovernment activity. Deschutes County was not exempt, and I was informed that a member of Posse Comitatus was accused of sexually assaulting a younger family member. I was asked to attempt an interview with this man, and although doing so sparked some additional concerns, I took it on as a challenge. Several deputies and I went to the suspect's home early in the morning, and I immediately made contact with him. I talked about his family's home and property and mentioned how lucky he was to be in such a location. We then talked a little bit about the length of time he had lived there and where the family had moved from. Then I said I was conducting an investigation and wanted him to come with me to the sheriff's office for an interview to assist in the investigation. He agreed, and I continued the friendly conversation all the way to the office.

Once we arrived, I took him into an interview room and read him the Miranda warning, and he agreed to talk with me. I used my usual approach, asking about his history. I don't recall his mentioning any specific abuse, but for whatever reason, he opened up and admitted to sexual contact with his family member. He said that he felt bad and wanted to get help. This was unlike anything I had expected from someone whom we believed to be an antigovernment activist, but I was happy to get the confession.

Once again I found myself before a judge and facing an attorney who accused me of violating his client's Fifth Amendment rights. This attorney also jumped all over the fact that I was friendly to his client and had talked with him about his current and past home before advising him of his rights. Like other judges, this judge found it a bit odd that an attorney from Portland would claim in a Deschutes County courtroom that Deschutes County deputies had violated constitutional rights by being nice. He was quick to deny the attorney's motion. That judge was later listed in bogus court filings as part of a criminal scheme to take away citizens' rights.

·   ·   ·

On July 11, 1997, I was called to investigate a murder-suicide. Upon my arrival at the scene, I learned that Debra Glazier, a forty-one-year-old nurse, had called 911 to report an intruder but the call was interrupted. Deputies were dispatched and met a vehicle as it left the scene. Inside the car Glazier was held at gunpoint by her ex-boyfriend, thirty-seven-year-old Michael Murphy. As deputies approached, Murphy shot and killed Glazier and then turned the gun on himself. This was devastating to the families and to the responding deputy, who, although he did everything he could, felt helpless.

. . .

In the early morning hours of July 19, 1997, I was called out to a stabbing in the Whispering Pines area, halfway between Bend and Redmond. Upon my arrival, I learned that an unknown assailant had attacked a woman with a knife. During the commotion, three of the woman's friends came to her aid, and all three were also stabbed. Lawrence McVey was stabbed in the abdomen and was the only one who would not recover from his wounds. As suddenly as he had appeared, the attacker left. A pickup belonging to William Knight was found a short distance away, but Knight was nowhere around.

A short time after the stabbing, a sergeant found William Knight standing by a fire along Highway 97. It appeared that he had crossed an irrigation canal between the home of the stabbing and Highway 97 and had started a fire to dry himself off. I was a short distance away, and so I went to the fire and asked that Knight accompany me to the sheriff's office. He agreed, but he had very little to say. When the sergeant mentioned how handy Knight was with a knife since he was able to stick four people before any of them even knew what was going on, Knight just laughed.

During initial interviews, we had received Knight's description and name, and those we interviewed said he was possibly involved only because some of those at the home had been introduced to him by a friend of theirs. The friend was Knight's girlfriend, and Knight had given her and her boys a ride from Washington to Bend.

Getting anyone to say they knew for sure Knight was the stabber or why he had attacked them became next to impossible. This case was not the first in which many of those with knowledge had run-ins with the police, which made it tricky to get them to admit what they knew since they felt they'd be labeled as snitches.

I visited a home where I believed Knight's girlfriend had fled after the assault. Police had been here on several prior occasions, so I anticipated the visit to be a dead end. Once there, I explained that I wanted to come in to talk about the stabbing. The people there said they knew nothing but that I was free to come in. They offered me a cup of coffee, which I accepted. It was a pleasant blend of coffee, and I complimented them on it. This took them back—they had not expected this from a cop. At the end of our conversation, they said they had received a phone call about the incident. The caller told them that on the night of the stabbing, Knight's girlfriend had called in a panic to say that she believed Knight thought she was having an affair with one of the residents of the home where the stabbing occurred. Knight hid in the shrubs, and in the darkness, he mistook the other woman for his girlfriend and then attacked this woman.

Next I visited the person who had allegedly received the call from Knight's girlfriend. She initially said she knew nothing about the stabbing. I then asked, "Is there any reason why we would have a tape of your phone conversation indicating you knew all about the stabbing?" Right away she said that she had known we had bugged the phone, and she agreed that the conversation had taken place.

In a couple days, I made a trip back to Whispering Pines, where I met with a great deal more cooperation. In the second interview, I was told that news of buggings was all over Whispering Pines, so residents wanted to come clean about what they knew. One of the victims also told me that a friend had told her that I had been over and shared a cup of coffee. The friend reassured her that I was a good guy and was particularly pleased that I hadn't looked in the cup before drinking the coffee. This simple cup of coffee had greased the wheels for even more cooperation than I had ever expected.

When it came time for the murder trial, many of the witnesses wanted to back out and some even changed their stories. I was glad that I had recorded some of those early interviews and felt that we still had a good case, but since no knife was ever found and since Knight claimed that he had used the knife in self-defense, the case was not a slam dunk.

On day two of the trial, Knight's attorney offered to plead guilty to manslaughter, two counts of second-degree assault, and one count of first-degree assault. Knight was sentenced to 165 months, and as far as I could tell, most of the victims and their families were satisfied with the outcome. I also can't help but think that many of those who did cooperate were glad they didn't have to get on the stand and be viewed as snitches.

.   .   .

In 1998, I was working another child-abuse case, and I received a shocking piece of information when I asked those who were around the child if they had any concerns about others with access to the child. One person provided insight into a family that had been around this child, explaining that he had heard a rumor about a missing-persons case from 1976. He said that the missing girl, Suzie, was found dead near where this family had lived. After seeing what had happened to the child I was investigating, he now wondered if there wasn't something to the rumor that Suzie was raped and killed by one if not two of the brothers in the family.

I wasn't aware of a case like the one he had described, but I immediately returned to the office to talk with my sergeant, who had worked for the sheriff's office for nearly thirty years. He quickly said that the man was talking about Suzanne Wickersham. On July 11, 1973, Suzanne, a seventeen-year-old Bend girl, had dropped a car off for her mother at the downtown drugstore. Suzanne was last seen at eleven thirty at night walking in the direction of her home. The initial missing/runaway report was short, only half a page. As anyone can imagine, the loss of the girl, who had her entire life in front of her, devastated the family.

I pulled the reports and learned that Deschutes County picked up the case on January 20, 1976, when a hiker located human remains just south of Bend near the Highway 97 scale house, just east of an area called DRW, for Deschutes River Woods. DRW was also the home of that case's suspect, his parents, and his brother. The medical examiner identified the remains as being Suzanne Wickersham and the cause of death as a gunshot to the head. The report further indicated that the entrance wound was consistent with a small-caliber bullet, possibly a .38.

The suspect had quite a lengthy juvenile record. The reports listed him as a suspect in attempted kidnapping, at gunpoint, of a Bend community-college librarian. He later attempted to kidnap another young woman, also with a gun, while she was walking in downtown Bend. Juvenile courts let him go with probation and ordered that he seek treatment.

In 1998, I talked with several of the suspect's friends, and they told me that he was obsessed with sex. He talked about his desire to rape women and also about his fascination with murder. They regularly visited strip clubs in Portland, and these trips seemed to increase his sexual appetite. The suspect was married in 1973 but later divorced. His ex-wife told us that he was messed up. She said that he would come home and rape her like a stranger. He would tie her up, place a bag over her head, and force himself on her. At that time he was working nights for the railroad, she said, and when not working, he would stay out at all hours.

On July 2, 1973, one week before Suzanne disappeared, a Pennsylvania couple on their honeymoon were traveling through Oregon and pulled off Highway 97 at the scale house. Around three in the morning, they woke to a man banging on their van. The man demanded that the woman step out of the van naked or he said he would start shooting. The couple immediately started the van and took off on the most direct route back to the highway. Just then, shots rang out, and the van was struck by several bullets. In the panic, the van got stuck in rough terrain. The couple ran from the van toward the highway. They reported that they ran about half a mile before a passing motorist, in a white Jeep pickup, stopped to offer them a ride.

The driver told the Pennsylvania couple that he worked for the railroad and was on his way to work. They said that they noticed a rifle in a gun rack, and the driver's comments and behavior made the hairs stand up on the backs of their necks. They asked to be dropped off at the first business in Bend, where they then called the Oregon State Police (OSP).

OSP reports indicated that .38-caliber bullets were recovered from inside the couple's van, but no other evidence was located that could identify the suspect. These reports also indicated that on a separate occasion, this suspect had been questioned while out target shooting with a .38-caliber revolver in a small rock pit just east of the scale house, in the general area where the Pennsylvania couple had stopped to spend the night and where Suzanne Wickersham's remains were found in 1976.

On October 16, 1973, a twelve-year-old-girl got off the school bus in a small subdivision east of Bend near Alfalfa. The child was walking home on the gravel road when a man in white pickup pulled up to her, pointing a handgun at her, ordered her in the truck. She complied and was taken down an isolated road, where she was raped. After completing his sexual act, the man pointed the gun at her but didn't pull the trigger. He then drove off as if nothing had happened. The girl wrote the license plate number in the dirt, went home, and immediately OSP was called. The license number in the dirt, although off by one digit, belonged to this same suspect's white Jeep pickup.

OSP contacted the suspect, who broke down during their interview. He admitted to raping the girl and added he had problems and could not control his sex drive. OSP made no connection to Suzanne Wickersham, who was believed to be a runaway at this time, or the Pennsylvania couple, but the suspect was arrested on a charge of first-degree rape, and a .22-caliber revolver was collected and determined as the weapon involved.

After Suzanne Wickersham's remains were located in 1976, there was a great deal of suspicion that this suspect, who was now confined in the state penitentiary in Salem, was responsible for her murder. The sheriff's office executed a search warrant but found no .38. The suspect's father said that his son had owned a .38 but had sold it to transients in a van out by the rock pit near the scale house. Investigators went to the state pen, where they asked the suspect if he would take a polygraph regarding Suzanne Wickersham's murder. He declined, and the detectives never attempted to question him again. The suspect completed his sentence for the rape of the 12 year old and was released a few months later.

Work records indicated that this suspect had failed to show up for his scheduled shifts on July 2, July 11, and July 12, 1973. Police reports also indicated that this same man was suspected of stealing from the railroad, but nothing was ever proved.

I returned to question my informant and probe for additional details. He told me that the suspect and his brother used to bury items between their house and the carport. They kept them buried until they believed the suspicion was off and then would sell or use the items. The informant told us that he had heard rumors that the suspect's brother had raped his own child and forced another child to watch.

These allegations opened a whole new series of interviews. Reluctantly, family members confirmed that rapes had taken place and that the father would have his son watch, under the pretext of teaching the boy about sex. We obtained a phone tap, and with our additional interviews about activities surrounding the 1973 murder, we were convinced that key family members would be talking. During one of the conversations, the brother was accused of being a part of the kidnap and murder. He denied it but said that his brother, the suspect, had committed the murder on his own, and the brother insisted that his only involvement was that he disposed of the .38.

We returned to the suspect's ex-wife to see if she could provide any additional insight. She said that while the suspect was in prison, she went to see him and asked him if he was responsible for Suzanne's death. She said he nodded yes but said nothing about it. When he got out of the pen, he began driving trucks. She recalled that when he returned from a trip along the Columbia River on the Washington side, he said that he had picked up a female hitchhiker. He told the ex-wife that he had tried to rape the hitchhiker, but she fought with him, and he ultimately dumped her out. This led the ex-wife to believe the hitchhiker may have been the victim of murder. Afterward, the suspect and his wife moved to the Portland area, and she lived in constant fear of ending up like Suzanne or the unknown woman in Washington. She added that around then, the Green River task force (a multi-agency investigation team looking into dozens of deaths of Oregon and Washington women, whose bodies were then disposed of along the Green River), was asking for tips, and she then decided to leave her husband and call the task force to report her suspicions.

While we talked with the brother's daughter, who now had a family of her own, she also brought up that, because of her father's deviant sex drive and odd behavior, she believed he was responsible for several unsolved homicides in the Portland area. It appeared both brothers were suspected, by their own family members, of being serial killers. Other family members said that the parents went to their graves believing their son was responsible for Suzanne's death. The information also came out that although the brother denied having any part in the murder he had gone to the pen with his father and during their visit confronted the suspect, who admitted he was responsible for Suzanne's death.

We decided to contact the owners of the home where this family had lived and had possibly buried items. We located old tires and plastic sheets with rust spots on them, apparently from tire rims—the suspect was believed to have stolen tires—but we were unable to locate any items linking the brothers to any missing persons or homicide case.

We then decided to attempt interviews with the brother, now living in Arkansas; the suspect, living in Portland; and each of their children. The plan was to start with brother and gain his cooperation in making a recorded phone call to the suspect. The district attorney made it clear that no arrest should be made without a full confession or the district attorney's prior approval. The sergeant agreed.

The detectives met with the brother, and after initial denials, he admitted that his brother had confirmed that he was responsible for Suzanne's death. The brother also retrieved a set of pistol grips and said that the suspect asked him to dispose of the gun after the brother learned of the murder. The brother said that although they told police that they had sold the gun to some transients, he had actually ground up the metal portion of the gun but saved the grip. He also said that he had further evidence to prove his brother was responsible, and the brother explained that he shot the gun into the ground and a tree trunk just outside the back door of their DRW home. The brother believed we could retrieve the bullets and then match them with the one from Suzanne.

When we asked him if he would make a phone call to his brother, he refused, saying that he would not be responsible for sending his brother away for the rest of his life. Upon further pressure, he feigned heart problems and said he needed medical help.

It was now time for my interview with the suspect. I had obtained a court order allowing me to secretly record our conversation, and the OSP detective and I waited for him to return home from his truck-driving job. I met him in the driveway and explained that I was part of a task force investigating the cold case of Suzanne Wickersham and asked if he would answer some questions. He agreed, and we made our way inside and sat at the kitchen table.

I began by asking him questions about his past. I brought up the attempted kidnappings and rapes, and he said he had no memory of those incidents. I also brought up the twelve-year-old girl, and he said he did remember that incident. I asked if he recalled the incident of the Pennsylvania couple being shot at. He said he didn't remember it. I told him I believed he had selective memory, as I would remember if someone had been shot at less than a quarter mile from my home. I also said that it was hard for me to believe that he didn't remember using a gun to kidnap two separate women.

I asked if he had given the couple from Pennsylvania a ride into town, noting that they had described his pickup and him and even said that the driver told them he worked for the railroad. I asked if there could have been any reason why they gave his license plate number as the one on the vehicle that gave them a ride. He said he could have given them a ride, but he just didn't remember doing so.

I asked him to tell me what he knew about Suzanne, dropping a picture of her down in front of him. He immediately got up, poured out his glass of ice water, went to the refrigerator for new ice, poured fresh water, and then sat back down to say he didn't know anything about her. I then said his family believed that he was responsible for Suzanne's death, and he agreed that his father went to his grave believing that.

We were interrupted by his new wife's return from work. An OSP detective took her into a separate room to interview her. I then questioned the suspect again about his history, asking if he felt he ever got the treatment he needed after the assaults and attempted kidnappings he committed as a juvenile, and he said no. He explained that although he had been ordered to undergo treatment, there was never any follow-up from the state requiring that he complete the treatment. I asked if he believed that the lack of treatment had resulted in his acting out in inappropriate ways, and he said yes. I asked if he believed he still was having problem, and he said yes.

I told him that I knew he was responsible for Suzanne's death. He looked down at his lap and not at the picture. I said that I believed he was only acting out in response to things that were done to him, and just as he told the trooper after raping the twelve-year-old Alfalfa girl, I believed his sex drive was out of control. His first words were; "Yes" and then said; "What my brother and uncle did to me really messed me up." I repeated this theme to pressure him into admitting the murder but was interrupted by shouts coming from the back of the house. His wife yelled for him to shut up, screaming that we were trying to put him away for life. The state police detective managed to escort her outside, and I tried to resume my line of questioning, but he stopped talking, got up, poured out his ice water, and then refilled his glass as he had done before.

He returned to the table and more strongly denied having any knowledge about Suzanne's death. He acted as though he had cooperated fully and needed us to leave. I tried to appeal to his compassion by asking him how he would feel if his daughter had been kidnapped and murdered. Wouldn't he want the responsible party to admit the crime and apologize? He even more strongly insisted that our conversation was over.

The other investigator and I left, and I couldn't help but think I had made a mistake by interviewing the suspect in his home, where he could get up and get a glass of water to reduce his anxiety and strengthen his resolve whenever the stress got too great. I also realized that using compassion had been a mistake. I should have known from how he treated his own children that he had no compassion and so this approach was doomed. I also believe that if he were arrested, he would have given an admission, just as he had done after each of his other arrests. I also heard that after we left he and his wife moved items from his home, thinking we may be back with a search warrant. I couldn't help but think, had we gone in with a search warrant we may have found his trophies or keepsakes from Suzanne's or possibly some other victim's death.

We returned to Bend and tried to strengthen our case in other ways. We sent the grips off to the lab in hopes of finding DNA, and we excavated the area outside the back door of their previous home, but we found no bullet. We took the case to the district attorney's office and pleaded that they take the case before a grand jury, but they wouldn't for fear of losing the case, claiming we didn't have enough evidence for a conviction. I know any one of the people investigating this case would have preferred to present what evidence we did have before a grand jury to let them decide; however, we police don't control that process. I am still stuck trying to figure out how no justice could be found for these crimes. Suzanne's father became an alcoholic and died a young man, her mother also died relatively young, and other family members said neither ever recovered from their loss. I can't help but think of the ending of the book *Mind Hunter*, by FBI profiler John Douglas, who put it simply: "Sometimes the dragon wins."

Chapter Ten

Tequila Shots

February 7, 1997, the sheriff's office was dispatched to the hospital, where a twenty-four-year-old La Pine woman reported that she was the victim of a sex crime. Detectives were soon present, and the young woman gave some details but left out a lot because she just couldn't remember everything. She recalled going to a Bend nightclub and seeing some of her friends hanging out with a man in a Lincoln. She met him and thought he seemed nice, so she agreed to have a tequila shot with him.

The man retrieved the tequila and orange slices from the trunk of the Lincoln and offered the friends drinks. The woman recalled having a couple of drinks with him, but then things started getting fuzzy. By this time, her friends had gone back inside the club, leaving her alone with the man. She awoke early the next morning in the Lincoln a few blocks from her home. She realized her bra was missing, her blouse was on backward, and her breasts were extremely sensitive, almost raw, like they had been aggressively rubbed. She knew that she had not agreed to any sexual contact. The man, who now seemed upset with her, asked her where she lived and then dropped her off at her home.

She knew this was not like her. She said she had never had blackouts from drinking alcohol, and she just didn't become intimate with men she didn't know. She decided to go to the hospital in hopes that evidence could be gathered that would prove she was, in fact, drugged and raped.

We spoke with a few of her friends and learned that the man was from Redmond and involved in photographing participants in the rodeo circuit. We contacted Bend and Redmond Police and learned that the suspect was Richard Coym, a pudgy forty-two-year-old man with glasses, a receding hairline, and a beard. We also learned this was not the first time he had been accused of drugging and raping a woman.

In November of 1991, Redmond Police received a report from a woman who said that Coym had offered her a ride home, but once she was in the car, he drove in the wrong direction, so she tried to jump from the car. He pulled her back in, but she feared for her life, so she tried to jump out a second time and succeeded in getting away. Coym said her activity was the result of her intoxicated state. Believing they did not have enough evidence to proceed with a case, police took no further action.

Redmond police received two additional calls in 1991 from women believing that Coym had sexually assaulted them, but because no evidence could validate their complaints, police initiated no criminal proceedings. Complaints again came in in April 1995, June 1996, and August 1996. In each case, women reported that they believed they were drugged then raped by Coym. Unfortunately, investigators looked at each case on its own merit rather than as a series of related cases, and because most of the woman had problems recalling details, the women, to avoid public ridicule, chose not to move forward with criminal charges. Coym was interviewed in each case, and each time he denied drugging the woman but admitted to consensual sexual intercourse. Still another time, the police were called to Coym's neighborhood, where a half-naked and extremely intoxicated woman was wandering through the neighborhood. When the police arrived, they found Coym helping the woman back to his house. He described her as his girlfriend and assured police that he would not allow her to further endanger herself and would make sure she didn't go out again.

We made a trip to the nightclub where the La Pine woman had clear memories of walking to his car and sharing orange slices and tequila shots. Exactly where she described the car had been parked, we found a half-dozen orange peel slices. We also conducted a criminal history check on Coym and learned that he had spent ten years in the state prison between 1974 and 1988 on several convictions for rape, sex-abuse, and drug charges.

Further investigation found that he had trained and worked as an EMT, so we believed he would have a better than average understanding of medication and its effects. We also learned that around 1989, after being released from prison, he had moved to Central Oregon. We realized that since his release, although not being arrested, he had far from walked the straight and narrow.

My job turned toward drafting a search warrant. We had a lot of information from which to draw a lot of conclusions about the types of trophies, photos, or drugs that he may still have in his Lincoln and house. Our goal was to have a search warrant in hand by February 13, and we put a team in place to follow Coym and watch for an attempt to pick up any women. When that happened, the team would step in, search warrant in hand, and hopefully catch him with the alcohol and drugs.

I worked hard to complete the warrant and had the district attorney's office standing by to review it. Unfortunately, the warrant needed too many changes, so we called off the surveillance team. I spent most of the night adding to the warrant, and by early the next morning, the DA was ready to have the judge review it. It was February 14. *How appropriate*, I thought, *that we would take down this sexual predator on Valentine's Day.*

With the search warrant in my pocket, I went to Coym's home in Redmond and made initial contact with him. I asked if I could come in and speak with him, and he allowed me in. I explained that I was there to talk with him about allegations of unwanted sexual contact and that I needed to advise him of his rights, which I did. I wouldn't have been shocked if he had invoked his rights, but I believe he had become accustomed to police interviews and successfully avoiding any charges and therefore agreed to speak with me.

I chose not to begin the search right away but rather to continue with my noncustodial interview in hopes of gaining admissions. I brought up investigators' knowledge of his past crimes and his treatment in a postconviction program for sex offenders. I asked him his opinion of the program and whether he believed the system had helped him. He was quick to say that he believed there were problems with the program and its ability to truly help those in need. I asked, "Do you believe you're still experiencing some problems because of the system's failure to treat you?" He replied, "Yes."

This was the ice breaker. I was a little confused about how I could be gaining admissions so quickly, but I didn't want to look a gift horse in the mouth. I praised him for his honesty and then asked him if he had been having problems for long, and he said yes. I asked him if he could give me an idea of how many women may have been affected by his problems, and he said about four different women.

I then asked for him to tell me about them, and he provided me with two names. He said he felt bad for one of them because he believed he may have taken advantage of her in her intoxicated state. He described the second woman as a friend, and he told me that after they had relations, she accused him of taking advantage of her. I pulled out a piece of paper and drew a line on it and then drew a perpendicular line dividing the first line in half. I explained that society views behavior on a continuum from completely acceptable to completely unacceptable behavior and that the dividing line was where society separated acceptable and unacceptable behavior. I pointed out that the left side of the divider was acceptable behavior, and then I made a small X on the extreme right side. I said that this X was where the activity of Jeffrey Dahmer fell. Coym said he knew who Dahmer was and acknowledged that he understood the difference between acceptable and unacceptable behavior. I gave him my pen and asked him to place a mark on the line where he believed his behavior with these two women fell. He moved about a third of the way from center line toward the X on the right and made his mark.

Then I asked him if he would consent to a search of his home and Lincoln, and he agreed and signed a consent form. I radioed for the search team to approach and pulled out our warrant, and after reading it to him, I asked if he would come with me to the sheriff's office to continue our conversation. He agreed. While the other detectives began the search, I took him to the office.

Back at the office, each time I brought up a victim, Coym agreed they had been drinking alcohol but denied providing them any drugs. He also admitted that maybe each woman believed the contact was unwanted, but he insisted that he believed it was consensual. I separated from him at one point to gather a DNA kit, and he consented to my swabbing his cheek. I then asked for a urine sample, and he invoked his rights. This, too, confused me. How could he be so helpful and then at the request for urine suddenly became uncooperative?

After charging Coym with sexual assault and kidnapping, with bail set at fifty thousand dollars, I returned to Coym's residence, where I learned that he had a secret compartment in his car door. Inside was a large shot glass coated on its side with pill residue and a film canister with what appeared to be drug residue covering its sides. Although he didn't live with any women, we found an extensive collection of female undergarments, some jewelry, and women's IDs in the house. We believed these to be trophies that would allow him to relive his conquests any time he chose.

It now appeared our investigation was truly just beginning. Although we had names of potential victims, we had not yet contacted them because we feared that word of our investigation would get out and Coym would destroy evidence. We decided to set up a hotline for potential victims, thinking that this may turn up a few additional victims. Little did we know that we would talk to hundreds of people, including dozens of victims. The majority of callers explained that they had heard about him and his offering drinks to women.

We learned that not only had police agencies never connected the dots between several prior reports but that most drinking establishments were also aware of Coym's activity. Most had heard about women becoming extremely ill, intoxicated, or incoherent after accepting his drinks, but although they had heard of these rumors, none had actually been validated by a formal complaint to them.

By February 21, we had talked with about one hundred different callers, four of whom were actual victims of rape in Deschutes County. Their stories all followed a pattern: The women agreed to have drinks with Coym and then immediately felt like they had been drugged. They awakened knowing that they had nonconsensual sex. One of the women was so convinced of the rape that she put the skirt she had been wearing in a paper sack and never wore it again. She believed we could find seminal fluid on it and offered it as evidence.

On the afternoon of the twenty-first, we received a call from the jail saying that Coym's parents were on their way with the 10 percent that would release him. We decided that we couldn't wait for a grand jury to hear the evidence and further charged Coym, the new charges were four counts of first-degree rape, four counts first-degree kidnapping, and four counts of first-degree sexual abuse. This increased his bail to four hundred thousand dollars.

As word of the case spread throughout Oregon, we got calls from woman all across the state reporting contact with Coym while attending rodeos such as the Pendleton Round-Up and St. Johns Rodeo or visiting local watering holes after the rodeos. Their reports bore an eerie similarity: he offered them drinks, and in many cases, they felt they had been drugged, and some believed they had been raped. We knew that Coym was a serial rapist. He found victims that were embarrassed and, because of the drugging, unable to recall exactly what happened, so he knew most would never want to testify.

In answering one of the hotline calls, I spoke with a woman who did not want to identify herself. She said that she had been out on February 13 and that Coym had offered her a drink. She couldn't recall much more of what happened until she found herself in his home early the next morning. She too believed that she had been drugged and raped, but because she was involved in a relationship, she had been unwilling to report it. I then connected her departure early on Valentine's Day with how cooperative Coym was when we first met. We had just missed seeing the victim depart, and Coym was probably panicking. I can only assume that Coym suspected she had made a report and that his worst fear—that a woman would make a report while physical evidence could still be detected—was coming true.

The DA's office moved forward to prosecute only the strongest cases, those of eight women from Deschutes County. On September 12, 1998, the trial finally began. DA Patrick Flaherty's opening statement to the jury of seven men and five women argued that the case was about deception and that evidence would show that Coym "preyed on women" and used alcohol and drugs to take advantage of them.

The defense attorney's opening statement argued that most of the women failed to report any wrongdoing, and in all of the cases, the women had been drinking, thus leaving them with clouded memories.

The first victim to testify was the La Pine woman, now twenty-six. She said that she did voluntarily have drinks in Coym's car, and she remembered that he had not made any advances toward her. She added that he made her feel comfortable. After her friends had left her alone with Coym, she had one more drink from the trunk of his car, and within five minutes, she was slumping in the seat and unable to keep her eyes open. She next recalled him shaking her awake and asking for directions to her home. She said her shirt was on backward and her bra was missing. She said that her breasts were red and raw and that she had bruises on her arms. She described feeling groggy all day and that finally she decided to go to the hospital, where she spoke to police.

A second victim, a thirty-five-year-old woman, spoke about an incident in December of 1994, when she and a female friend were having drinks at a local nightclub. She said that Coym bought them each a drink and then offered them free drinks of tequila from his car. They accepted, and after having a drink, the victim's friend passed out and the victim started to feel groggy. She recalled him starting the car and her telling him not to take them anywhere. She was unable to stop him and soon found herself and her friend at Coym's home. She said she could not stay awake and realized that she could not get away. She said that she later awoke to find Coym on top of her, having sex. She tried to push him off but was too weak and groggy. When she woke again later, Coym offered to take her and her friend back to their car, which he did. She said that because she was still groggy, she and her friend slept in her car. She clearly stated that neither of them agreed to go anywhere with Coym and that she never consented to sex.

The next victim, a forty-one-year-old Redmond woman, testified to meeting Coym in a Redmond bar in June of 1996. She said that after a few drinks, she left the bar and went to a nearby ATM. While she withdrew cash, Coym drove up as if he had been following her. She said he offered her a shot of tequila, which she accepted, within a matter of minutes, she passed out. She woke up five hours later in the street feeling like she had engaged in sex.

A forty-two-year-old from Hillsboro knew Coym as a rodeo photographer, and she ran into him in a Redmond bar in August of 1995. The woman had planned to stay at a motel, but Coym offered her a spare room, which she accepted. She said that Coym offered her a drink, but she wanted only a soda. She retrieved some items from her car and then finished the soda. She recalled feeling sleepy almost instantly and passing out. She woke up later in Coym's bedroom with the feeling that she was coming out of anesthesia. She testified that she knew sex had taken place, but she could not recall it.

A fifth victim, a thirty-six-year-old woman from Bend, recalled meeting Coym after a country dance lesson in February 1994. He offered her drinks of tequila while still in the bar. After returning from the bathroom, she finished her second drink. She then remembered waking up in the front seat of Coym's car with his hands on her breasts. She told him to stop, and he did, and he then returned her to her own car.

The victim who had saved her skirt with the semen stains chose not to testify, saying it would further complicate her life. Although we didn't get her testimony, we did get DNA matching the DNA collected from Coym in our tests of the skirt. The state brought in evidence of seven different prescriptions that Coym had in his possession. They included back and muscle relaxants and painkillers, but nothing more than pill binder had been identified on the shot glass, film canister or on a metal flask that was also collected. (An FBI expert later testified that Oregon crime labs required certain amounts of drugs to be present before they would confirm trace amounts but that their results didn't mean that no drugs were present. The expert also explained that the mixture of alcohol and some of the seized drugs produced the effects that all of the victims had described.)

I testified to my interview with Coym. The jury was very attentive when I spoke about his admissions that he had wronged the four women and his indication that his behavior was unacceptable to the public by making his mark on the line I had drawn.

The defense team then tried to paint the picture of intoxicated couples engaging in behavior that was consensual but that the victims had chosen to believe they happened against their will because of their intoxication. One of the experts called by the defense was presented with the shot glass. The defense attorney asked if this was a large shot glass, and the expert said it was larger than a single shot. On cross-examination, the DA asked the defense expert about the residue, which could still clearly be seen on the glass. The expert responded by saying it appeared to be pill binder and described that binder was the material left behind when prescription drugs were dissolved in liquids.

On September 22, the case was sent to the jury. Less than four hours later, the jury returned with a verdict of guilty on all twenty-one counts of rape, kidnapping, and sexual assault. On October 6, 1998, Judge Tiktin told Coym, "Your predatory days are over" and then sentenced him to 102 ½ years in prison.

Chapter Eleven

District Commander

In the spring of 1998, I completed a promotion-assessment center, and although I was selected for a district commander position, I was told that I would be promoted only after budget concerns were addressed in the fall elections. The sheriff's levy was approved in the October election and I was promoted to sergeant and took the position as the North Bend district commander. My new responsibilities included activities on the north side of Bend and in the communities of Alfalfa and Tumalo along with supervising all of Deschutes County when no other sergeant was on duty. My work schedule, because I was the least senior of three sergeants, was ten-hour shifts, days on Wednesday and Thursday and then swings on Friday and Saturday.

During the early morning hours of July 27, 1999, I received a call from dispatch and told that deputies were responding to a reported triple homicide in the small community of Tumalo. Within twenty minutes, I was on scene and informed that the suspect, Robert Lawrence Staudinger, had pulled into the parking lot at the Deschutes County Sheriff's Office jail and told deputies over the intercom that he had killed some people and wanted to turn himself in. The deputy on duty spoke to Staudinger, who had blood on his clothes and said that three people were dead in his Tumalo home. Additional deputies were sent to the address, and when I arrived, they had just confirmed the three deaths.

As the story unfolded, we learned that Staudinger was addicted to methamphetamine and suffered from meth paranoia. At about ten thirty in the evening on July 26, he got into an argument with his roommate, fifty-one-year-old Sharon Morris, and he ultimately shot her twice with a .22-caliber rifle.

Shortly after Staudinger killed Morris, twenty-seven-year-old Michael Morton and his friend, twenty-two-year-old Dawn Phillips, pulled up to the house. Staudinger was afraid that he would be caught, so he invited Morton inside and shot him once and fatally stabbed him in the neck. Staudinger then motioned to Phillips, who was waiting in the vehicle, to come inside.

Once Phillips was in the house, Staudinger attacked her with a knife, ultimately stabbing her nearly three dozen times. Staudinger said he had gone berserk, and it was hard not to agree with him when I learned that he had tried to clean up Phillips's body so that he could use it for sexual gratification. He had considered arson to cover up the homicides, but instead he chose to turn himself in. That was how he ended up at the jail intercom.

Staudinger never backed away from his confession, and although there was some delay during his mental health evaluations, in 2001, he pleaded guilty to seven counts of aggravated murder and one count of abuse of a corpse, guaranteeing that he would spend the rest of his life behind bars.

.   .   .

I worked a day shift on September 25, 1999, and being the only supervisor on duty, I went to assist the only La Pine deputy serve a felony warrant. Once I arrived in La Pine, dispatch advised of an attempted kidnapping of two young girls in the Redmond area. The details indicated that a man in a rust-colored van had pulled up to the girls' yard and tried to grab one of them. She successfully evaded his grasp and made the 911 call.

I informed the La Pine deputy that the warrant would have to wait because I was going to head toward Redmond. Shortly after the initial call, one of the Redmond deputies, who had a trainee with him, spotted a rust-colored van in front of a minimarket on the north end of Redmond. I later learned that the two deputies chose to wait for the driver to return to the van, and as soon as a man approached it, they yelled at him to stop. He refused to obey their orders and dashed toward the van, and one of the deputies chased him. The man jumped into the driver's seat, and the deputy reached through the open window to grab the keys. The suspect pulled away from the market, the deputy holding on to the door for a short distance before giving up and jumping off.

The next radio message was the deputy's call that he was in pursuit. I felt helpless. Although I turned on my lights and siren, I knew that I could only assist by radio. A second deputy from the north district advised that he was in Terrebonne, and I instructed him to stop traffic and deploy a spike strip on Highway 97. He was in the process of stopping traffic, yet, because of the speed of the approaching pursuit, he was unable to access the strip before the van arrived. The van didn't just pass by; rather, it drove directly into oncoming traffic and veered toward the deputy. The pursuing deputy kept everyone apprised of the van's speed and activities, including attempting to run over the other deputy and then driving head-on into oncoming traffic. I instructed the pursuing deputy to continue with lights and siren but to back way off, keeping a visual on the van but not pushing him into traffic.

The pursuing deputy confirmed that he had backed off and then said that the van had also slowed down. The driver now had his arm out the window and was motioning for the patrol car to come forward. The slowed pursuit pulled into the Peter Skene Ogden Wayside at the high bridge bordering Deschutes and Jefferson counties. I was relieved, as I knew that this was a single entry and exit rest area, and if we blocked the highway access, the van would have no way out. The first patrol car stopped at the entrance and prepared the spikes while the second vehicle followed the van into the rest area.

The next radio message was the second deputy saying, "He drove off the cliff." The suspect drove onto a railroad access road, between two large boulders, positioned just far enough apart for the van to squeeze through, and then accelerated, plunging nearly three hundred feet to the Crooked River below.

The investigation that followed revealed that thirty-three-year-old Steven Grogg had been despondent after his girlfriend left him and his dog died that same morning. His mother had called in to report that he was distraught, suicidal, and in possession of a gun. Fortunately, the girls he attempted to kidnap were able to get away and no one else was injured in the pursuit that followed.

. . .

On October 4, 1999, my family had just moved into our new home on five acres, and I was working in the yard when two patrol sergeants visited. I was pleased that they had come out to see my new home, but my emotions quickly changed when I learned that they were there to inform me that my father had died from a heart attack.

The funeral service was held in Wallowa County. Just as at Frank Ward's funeral, the sheriff's honor guard and a single bagpipe player, who bellowed out "Amazing Grace," were in attendance. The size of the audience was overwhelming, representing how well liked my father had been during his time as sheriff. During the service, I was asked if I wanted to say anything, but I found talking impossible. I felt that I needed to be strong like my father had always been and not show my emotions, but I couldn't keep the tears back.

. . .

As a patrol sergeant I often made split-second decisions that would be reviewed and questioned by command the following Monday morning. I made one such decision during a busy day shift. We had a major accident that tied up several patrol deputies and at the same time as I responded to a homicide investigation. When detectives relieved me from the homicide scene, I received a call about a found pipe bomb. I was the closest unit, so I responded. A rural resident had dug up an old pipe bomb in his field and decided to move it to the corner of his property. Unfortunately, this corner bordered two main roads, and the current protocol was to shut down all traffic within three hundred feet of the device and wait up to ten hours for the Salem bomb-disposal team to arrive and detonate it in place.

Knowing that our resources were already spread thin, I reverted to the bomb protocol I had successfully followed in La Grande. I picked up the device, placed it in the trunk of my car, and drove it to a secure and isolated location. I made sure to tell all employees that they were never to do the same, and although it worked out okay for me, I did find myself in front of the captain's desk the following Monday.

.   .   .

Y2K was fast approaching, and our department participated in several meetings to prepare for potential terrorist acts. I had all of the deputies develop lists of potential targets and methods of how to best use our resources to protect them. Because Central Oregon had been targeted in previous attacks, we wanted to be ready and watching for any possible terrorist acts on Y2K.

In the past several years, we had seen numerous terrorist activities related to Animal Liberation Front (ALF) and the Earth Liberation Front (ELF). On October 28, 1996, on Highway 22 between Bend and Salem, the Detroit Ranger Station had been the target of arson attempt. Trucks had been set on fire and spray-painted with "Earth Liberation Front." Later an incendiary device, which failed to ignite, was found on the roof of the ranger station's office. The damage was estimated to cost $21,500.

October 30, 1996, on Highway 58 between La Pine and Eugene, there was another arson, this time at the Oakridge Ranger Station. It too was linked to ELF, and this time the damage was estimated to cost $5,074,189.

July 21, 1997, there was an arson at Cavel West, a horse-rendering plant in Redmond, leaving a total loss of $1,211,388. A few days after the fire, the Animal Liberation Front sent a communiqué claiming responsibility for the Cavel West fire.

I wasn't scheduled to work on New Year's Eve, but because of the lack of supervision, I chose to work an additional shift. I made sure that all of our deputies were in the field and checking potential targets, but as night turned into morning, it appeared we had escaped any major event.

Unfortunately I was wrong. East of Bend, still in Deschutes County off Highway 20, a Bonneville Power Administration (BPA) electrical-power transmission tower had been the target of terrorists. We later learned that Jacob Ferguson, Stanislas Meyerhoff, Josephine Overaker, and Chelsea Gerlach, all ELF members, had planned to interrupt power between the Bonneville Dam and Los Angeles, California, by toppling one of the main power lines. On December 31, 1999, at 8:53 p.m., the four suspects had driven to the remote site off of Highway 20 and loosened the nuts on two of the supporting guy wires. They worked at it long enough that the tower eventually fell. From published reports, I learned that the fall created an arc of electricity described as being "like lightning," and the suspects fled. The resulting destruction didn't cause any power outage because alternate lines were still functioning and able to take the load from the down line. It did, however, cause nearly $126,000 in damages.

Years later, when talking with FBI agents, I learned that Deschutes County was the site of the only domestic terrorist activity related to Y2K. Not something I wanted to be remembered for, but I believe it was outside my control.

.   .   .

In early 2000, a new sheriff was elected, and he brought in his own command staff and restructured the remaining supervision. One sergeant retired, one moved on to another agency, and a third gave up his stripes, leaving four sergeants. One of those was assigned to investigations, and I along with the other two were assigned as team supervisors, with another sergeant being promoted to fill in the fourth team. Each team was now assigned to work two twelve-hour day shifts followed by two twelve-hour night shifts and four days off. At the same time, the community-policing deputies were pulled from their communities and assigned to work as part of a team to be more responsive to calls and less focused on specific communities.

After the restructuring, I became connected with a family during a very trying time for them. I was the watch commander when a request for a death notification came in. I was to locate the elderly parents of a woman who had died of hypothermia after apparently falling while in some kind of intoxicated state. I located the couple at the Salvation Army store where they volunteered. While waiting to speak with them, I learned that they had previously been selected as volunteers of the year for Deschutes County, and when I passed on the devastating information, I discovered what a caring and giving couple they really were. Within a few months, I was at their home. This time the wife had returned from church to find that her husband, who was extremely ill, had committed suicide. My third visit came the next Christmas as other children and grandchildren were visiting their grandmother. During the visit, the grandmother collapsed from a heart attack. While waiting with the family for the funeral home to arrive, they told me how peaceful their loved one's passing was. They also informed me that they had heard about me and the compassion I had shown during the previous two tragedies. I found that working in this community, even now that the population had risen to just over one hundred thousand, still allowed a deputy to become familiar with families and to make a difference.

. . .

On November 17, 2000, our office received reports of a subject going home to "blow his brains out." Our deputy responded and made sure the subject was taken to the hospital for a mental evaluation. The following day, the doctor saw the subject and released him with some medication. On November 19, this subject again told friends that he was going to kill himself, but our office received no additional call. On November 20, we did receive a call, and this time the subject had died from a single gunshot wound. I was working as the Bend sergeant, and after talking with the detective supervisor, I responded to act as the deputy medical examiner.

The subject's cabin was basically one large living area with the kitchen on one side and a couch and coffee table on the other side and a loft above. The deceased was found sitting back on the couch with a rifle between his legs and feet propped between the coffee table and couch. Investigators also found a note that didn't make complete sense. It said, "I didn't do it" but included "I love you" and a message to take care of his daughter and dog.

The deceased's head had exploded. From my experience, I knew this trauma would only be caused if the gun was in direct contact with the deceased, and this would cause the expanding gases to be more destructive than the actual bullet. Blood mist and brain matter had settled throughout the living room and kitchen area. The gun and ammo belonged to the deceased and had been retrieved from the loft. There were no injuries or displaced items to indicate a struggle had taken place, and the blood spatter was consistent throughout the house, indicating that no one had stood near the explosion, because if they had, there would have been a shadow where the debris hit them and not the items in the room.

I asked the deputy to contact both the medical examiner and district attorney, who is in charge of the medical examiner program. After hearing the details, they authorized the release of the body to the funeral home. The medical examiner viewed the body later at the funeral home to complete his investigation and sign the death certificate.

I had tried to make sure deputies located the next of kin and notified them, in person, of the death. While we were still at the cabin, the mother of the deceased arrived at the scene, and I asked how she had learned of the death, explaining that we had been trying to send someone to her. She said that a friend had called her. The mother explained that her son had been upset with her. He had recently offered to pay for round-trip tickets anywhere she wanted to go and she responded to his offer by saying she didn't want anything from him. He followed this up with a letter to his mom explaining how mean she had been. The mom was aware of his threats to harm himself and his recent mental health problems, but she was frustrated at the doctors for giving him medication, which she believed made the problems worse, and for releasing him.

Shortly after this investigation, I received word that the family was now claiming that their son was murdered and that they believed the police were involved in a cover-up. Specifically, they said that I had a girlfriend involved in the drug trade in La Pine, and they suggested that the death was related to information that the deceased had about corrupt officers. In previous suicide investigations, I found that it was not uncommon for family members to believe the victims to be incapable of killing themselves or causing the family the resulting pain. In these previous cases I had heard theories ranging from accidents to homicides, but usually in time, these claims dissipated.

In 2002, I received copies of e-mails describing the family's own investigation that claimed that I had a meth-dealing girlfriend in La Pine and that "everyone in La Pine knew Decker was corrupt." These claims caused me a great deal of anxiety. I had given my life to doing the best job I could, and now these false claims were making it impossible for me to sleep. All I could think about was just how many people would be hearing and believing these lies.

On April 9, 2002, I received an e-mail addressed as if it were from the deceased. The e-mail said, "Heard you on the radio this morning .   .   . bones found are being treated as criminal investigation. How do you know bones did not commit suicide?? Have a nice day!"

I spoke with an attorney about the harassment and slander but learned that the courts generally allowed for some acting out on the part of grieving family members, so he gave the advice that I should just ignore it. The family's lies continue to this day, and a website is still up with false claims about a conspiracy and my failure to properly investigate a homicide.

. . .

On March 26, 2001, a deputy was busy following leads on five teens who had taken one of their parents' cars and were planning to leave the area. These teens—Adam Thomas, eighteen; Justin Link, seventeen; Seth Koch, fifteen; Lucretia Karle, sixteen; and Ashley Summers, fifteen—would later be called the Redmond Five.

On the afternoon of March 26, the Redmond Five had gone to Adam Thomas's Tumalo-area home while his mother, fifty-two-year-old Barbara Ann Thomas, was at work. They had arrived at the home in Koch's parents' 1993 Cadillac and were making plans to go to Canada to start a new life. The problem they faced was that while at the Thomas residence, they misplaced the keys to the Cadillac and now needed another vehicle.

Who could ever believe the evil plan they then devised to get another vehicle? All five participated in the discussion. Lucretia Karle suggested that they fill the bathtub with water, put Barbara Thomas in the tub, and drop a stereo and hair dryer in the water, electrocuting Thomas. Ashley Summers suggested that they knock Thomas out and then inject her with bleach.

Just after five o'clock, Barbara Thomas arrived home, where the Redmond Five were waiting for her to execute their plan. Her son repeatedly bludgeoned her over the head with wine bottles. To the shock of the Redmond Five, she wouldn't go down and actually started to stagger outside. At this time Justin Link started giving commands. They all stopped the assault and waited until they could convince Barbara that they were done and that she should return to the house. Then Justin instructed Seth Koch, who had a .308 rifle, to shoot her, and Koch did as he was told, putting a bullet in Barbara Thomas's head.

The Redmond Five then took the keys to Thomas's 1998 Honda, and they departed for Canada. Around that same time, that Thomas had arrived home, the deputy was closing in on the teens. A witness had said that Ashley Summers had called to say that she and the other four were at the Thomas home preparing to go to Canada. The deputy then had to respond to a priority call, but once that call was completed, just before seven o'clock, he and another sergeant arrived at the Thomas home. They saw the Cadillac parked out front. As they walked around the outside of the home, the deputy spotted what appeared to be blood and human flesh on the blinds. Now facing a potential medical emergency, the two deputies entered the home and found Barbara Thomas dead on the floor.

Investigators obtained a search warrant, and during the search, they found electrical cords strung into the bathroom and a hair dryer and radio plugged in. They also found a bottle of bleach and a syringe filled with a clear liquid sitting out and bloody wine bottles, all which were later determined to have been used or planned for use by the Redmond Five.

An attempt to locate was put out for the Honda with special interest at the border crossings, and it wasn't long before word came back that the Redmond Five had been detained in Washington at the Canadian border. Deputies and members of the multiagency homicide team were immediately dispatched, and as soon as they arrived, they began questioning the teens only to discover the grisly details of the plan and ultimate murder of Barbara Thomas.

Ultimately all five pleaded guilty. Adam Thomas, Seth Koch, and Justin Link received true life sentences, while Lucretia Karle and Ashley Summers each received sentences of twenty-five years in prison.

· · ·

The new sheriff continued to restructure the organization, promoting two lieutenants and placing them in charge of two teams each. One of the lieutenants had been the supervisor of investigations, so this left an opening for a sergeant in that department, and I was asked to fill that position. I agreed and was soon supervising five busy detectives.

Chapter Twelve

Never Forget

Recalling how I was caught off guard when I investigated a child-abuse case and became involved in the unsolved homicide case of Suzanne Wickersham, I wanted to make sure that every detective was fully aware of all missing-persons and unsolved homicide cases. Additionally, I wanted to make sure that none of the victims or their families were ever forgotten. To accomplish this, I assigned current detectives to each of those cases, cold or active, and gave them responsibility for continuing the investigation as time allowed. My first step was to check the archives to identify all of those cases and then put them on a large whiteboard hanging in the detective division.

The oldest unsolved homicide was from October 11, 1929, and the victim was Keith Irving Hamilton, a sixteen-year-old sheepherder who worked for Pat Reilly of Ashwood. Hamilton, who was herding sheep along the Deschutes River approximately three miles south of Bend, was found dead from a gunshot wound. The reports indicated that the area Hamilton was found in was believed to be the location of a still, and later investigation revealed that Charles Hamilton, Keith's father, may have provided information to the prohibition authorities. Both theories, that he came upon still operators or that a still operator wanted to send a message to his father, appeared to be related to prohibition.

. . .

There was a missing-persons report from 1967 that indicated that at about one thirty in the afternoon on November 22, Richard Walters left his vehicle, which had been parked at the Mount Bachelor—Elk Lake junction, on foot and was not seen again. The file contained a letter from 1980 that also indicated that Richard Walters was never seen or heard from after that walk.

. . .

The first cases to be placed on the whiteboard were the case of Susan Wickersham and the sad case of Baby Jane Doe. On May 20, 1986, while collecting trash from a Dumpster in Terrebonne, the garbage truck operator found the body of a newborn baby girl. This baby had been discarded in the dumpster near the Sun Spot Drive Inn, and no leads ever developed that would identify the child's mother.

. . .

On March 27, 1989, Angela Chan was seen with her husband, Bruce Chan, who was home on a four-day pass from the Marine Corps. Bruce later told investigators that he and Angela had spent the morning shooting clay pigeons in the Dry Canyon area, between Redmond and Sisters along Highway 126. Bruce also said that he had dropped her off at home in Redmond around two in the afternoon before he departed for Camp Pendleton. On March 29, Angela's family reported her missing, and her car was then found abandoned on Highway 126 at the Cline Falls junction, approximately seven miles from Dry Canyon. There were reports that the Chans' marriage was a turbulent one, with Angela previously having suffered a broken arm, and Angela having an affair with another man. These reports pointed toward Bruce Chan as the suspect, but as is often the case, without a body, the case went cold.

. . .

At two o'clock in the afternoon on June 9, 1999, Ron Nordstrom was reported to have departed a home on Northeast Yucca in

Redmond on his bike and never seen again. The report indicated that Ron was scheduled to testify for the state in September in a sex-abuse case. Also listed in the report was the refusal of the family to allow a search of the home. Without probable cause, a search warrant hadn't been obtained.

.   .   .

On June 18, 2001, Corwin Osborn was hiking in the Three Sisters Wilderness, starting at Devil's Lake Trailhead, with the intention of reaching the summit and then meeting family members at Lava Camp Trailhead. The meeting never took place, and Corwin was never located.

.   .   .

A more recent case, from September 27, 2001, listed Gary Alan Larsen as missing and last seen leaving Redmond for Madras on September 16, 2001. Gary and his white 1995 Dodge pickup were never located.

.   .   .

On February 9, 2002, with the whiteboard complete and detectives assigned to each of the cases, we were assigned a new missing-persons case. Kate Svitek, a twenty-two-year-old snowboarder, was reported missing from the slopes of Mount Bachelor. In this type of case, the investigations unit was assigned to check the residence, to check for credit-card activity, and to conduct follow-up interviews with those who had contact with Kate. Our investigation did not indicate any suspicious behavior, and from our point of view, Kate Svitek was on the mountain as all who knew her said she was.

This soon became a point of contention for our search-and-rescue teams. Because of their past success and effective search practices, they truly believed she could not be on the mountain. The sheriff too began to entertain the possibility of foul play, and I soon realized that the investigators and I were being viewed as not doing enough to locate her.

This investigation came to a sad conclusion on March 4, when Kate's body was found in a tree well about three-hundred yards from the top of the ski lift and less than one hundred yards from where she was last seen. The investigation revealed that she had fallen into the tree well and that snow and ice had fallen on top of her board, both trapping and concealing her.

Chapter Thirteen

Crystal Teardrops

On July 31, 2002, employees of the Bend Fred Meyers store called to report employee Brenda Kay Middlekauff as missing. Employees explained that Brenda had last been at work on July 18 but had failed to show up for any of her following shifts. They also explained that she had not been in to collect her paychecks and that the only call came on July 20 from her husband, Darrell Middlekauff, to say that his wife had to go out of town on a family emergency.

I was on my annual vacation spending time with my kids in the sheep barn at the county fair when I received the first call about this missing person. It didn't sound good, so I asked that the detectives be as thorough as possible with an interview and consented search of the home. The standard checks of credit and contact with family and friends were the next steps we needed to take.

I returned to work the following Monday and sifted through the reports. We had learned that Brenda, forty years old, was a widow who owned her La Pine home as well as other properties. Brenda worked in the day-care area at Fred Meyers, and all those who worked with her gave the impression that she enjoyed her work and coworkers. Brenda had met Darrell through a mutual acquaintance, and they were quickly married. We also learned that Brenda had just recently been to the dentist to have her wisdom teeth removed and had only been back at work for a few days before she went missing. Investigators contacted Brenda's family members in Missouri and

Texas, and all said it was unlike Brenda to not stay in contact, and they further stated that there had not been any family emergency.

The initial interview with Darrell Middlekauff had taken place at the La Pine home. He told investigators that he had returned home to find Brenda with a lesbian truck driver and that Brenda left him for her, taking very little with her. He also went into detail about how Brenda had continued to call the house and had even come by some time later.

The background on Darrell K. Middlekauff revealed a criminal history dating back to 1979, including an arrest in 1992 in Fairfield, California, on suspicion of kidnapping and sexual assault. He later was convicted of the kidnapping and sentenced to prison. In 1996, eleven days after his release from prison, Middlekauff again kidnapped a woman at knifepoint, this time forcing her to drive to Ripon, California, where he bound her hands and feet. He was ultimately arrested, and he pleaded guilty to carjacking and was sentenced to an additional five years in prison. According to court records, Middlekauff had admitted to using meth since the 1980s.

Shortly after leaving California, Middlekauff had ended up in an Oregon prison, and although he was still on parole in California, Oregon was now his home. He had met a man who knew Brenda Hill, and Middlekauff asked that he introduce him to her, hoping that Brenda would write to him while he was in jail. This introduction took place, and Brenda did write to Middlekauff and even allowed him to move into her La Pine home upon his release. Brenda's sister said that, against her wishes, they were married within a month after they met.

The investigation grew, and information came in suggesting Middlekauff was continuing his drug activities and involvement with other women. We even had information that from July 17 to July 20, the time frame of Brenda's disappearance, Middlekauff had put up a girlfriend in a Redmond motel. We did our due diligence and found that by the end of August, there were no activities on any bank accounts or phone accounts and no contact with friends or family.

The only person to report seeing Brenda was Darrell Middlekauff, and he maintained that he last saw her around the end of July.

On September 12, investigators executed search warrants for the La Pine residence and a storage facility in Bend rented by Middlekauff. The search of the storage facility revealed chemicals and lab equipment, and the search of the La Pine home included a team of cadaver dogs to help discover evidence of a body.

I talked with the dog handlers and learned that the dog had been involved in the search of Ward Weaver's property in Portland earlier in August. It had alerted handlers to a scent trapped in the air by an awning above a new cement pad. Ashley Pond's body was found under that pad inside a barrel. I found it interesting how accurate the dog was. Now, during our search, the handlers had a "soft alert" in the spare-bedroom closet and another in the back of Middlekauff's PT Cruiser. From what I understood, this alert could indicate that body fluids or a decomposing body had been in these areas for a short time. No other evidence or a smoking gun could be found to prove any homicide had taken place at the La Pine home.

However, we did have evidence of Middlekauff's drug activity, and he was soon arrested. He pleaded guilty to the drug charges, getting a sentence of twenty-five months.

We learned that Middlekauff had been meeting with a girlfriend at a La Pine cabin, and there were rumors that he may have buried evidence there. We obtained consent for a search, and on a hot day, we searched the cabin's property, including an old septic hole left after an outhouse was moved. This was not the kind of searching that interested anyone, but we believed it was necessary. By the end of the day, all of us were hot, tired, and in need of a shower. One of the detectives had found a discarded wig and displaying his unique since of humor decided to bury it near a woodpile, and he suggested a couple other detectives make another sweep for the hair to see their reaction. One of our values being a sense of humor, I agreed and directed a couple detectives to sweep the area one last time before we left for the day. Within a few minutes they had spotted the hair, and they approached me with the find. They were convinced that a body lay underground near the woodpile, and acting as if I were tired and uninterested, I said that we should just leave it, adding that the dogs would be coming back the next day and we could see how good they really were. I think the detectives truly believed I was suffering from heat exhaustion, and although they were hesitant, they insisted that something be done right then. The puzzled look on their faces was priceless. The other detectives who were aware of the wig laughed, and soon the two finders were aware that they were the victims of a prank and relieved to know I had not gone completely crazy.

On December 31, 2002, a probation officer indicated that Middlekauff, who was in our county jail, was asking to talk with me about the release of some of his property. The case agent was on vacation, and I was more than willing to assist by making contact with Middlekauff. I and another detective, a very fit person, went to the jail to meet with him.

Middlekauff sat on the side of the table closest to the door, I sat opposite him, and the other detective sat at the end of the table between us. I explained who we were and told Middlekauff we were there to get the list of items he wanted returned. He was immediately confrontational, saying that he believed I was spreading lies about him. I again explained why I thought we were there, and then he started talking about his truck and marriage license and saying he wanted a copy of the search warrant, then he again veered from the intended topic of the meeting. I cautioned that he was talking about criminal acts and that I needed to advise him of his rights, which I did. He said he understood them and went right back to talking about how he believed we were treating him unfairly.

I stopped Middlekauff and asked him if at any time during the course of his interviews with the police about Brenda being missing he had given us inaccurate or untrue information. Middlekauff said that he had given false information to everyone he talked to, adding that he knew that by doing this, all of the information would be inadmissible in any future proceedings. I asked specifically if he had lied to the police, and he said yes. I gave him the opportunity to be honest and tell me what the lies were and why he told them to us.

He used this as an opportunity to say, "You know the amount of money taken by Brenda was much greater than I first told you." He mentioned that money and gold was missing from the safe in their home. I tried to refocus Middlekauff on lies pertaining to where Brenda was or when he last saw her. He said, "You tell me what statement I made and why you think it's a lie and then I will give you the answer." I became more confrontational and said, "I am not going to spoon-feed you information." I added, "I know Brenda is dead and you are responsible for her death." Middlekauff said simply that he knew I believed that. I told him that I believed he had gone home to tell Brenda about his relationship with the other woman, which led to a fight that resulted in Brenda's death. Middlekauff responded with a fake laugh and leaned back in his chair and whipped his long hair back. He then said that he would never have a relationship with a woman who looked like the one I was accusing him of sleeping with.

I pointed out that we knew he had paid for the woman's motel room, and he stopped me with a loud, "What?" I repeated that I knew he had paid for her room at the Super 8. He again denied this. I told him we had the receipts, and he then agreed that he had paid for a room one time as a favor to another friend. After a few more denials, he finally admitted that he had paid for the motel on two separate occasions but made it clear that he did not have a relationship with that woman.

I explained that during a search of a cabin we had found a pair of ripped panties, and I asked Middlekauff if there would be any chance that we would find his DNA on them. Middlekauff again spat out, "What?" I repeated myself, and his next response was that he had sex with her one time but that he did not believe that to be an affair.

I asked if he had considered that this woman may have been using him and possibly messing with his mind. I explained that a witness had told us that he had pleaded with her, asking her to be straight with him and to not mess with his mind. Middlekauff again leaned back in his chair, laughed loudly, and whipped his hair back, saying that there was no way she could have ever messed with his mind. I asked him how many times she had called him crying and asking for his help. "What?" he said again, and I repeated myself, giving more specifics about a time when he had met her at this cabin. He then admitted to meeting this woman on that occasion and added that he knew one of Brenda's friends had followed him to the cabin. Middlekauff then said that the friend was part of the reason why things "were deteriorating at the end."

I explained that we also knew of his plan to move this woman into his and Brenda's La Pine home to start a porn website. Middlekauff again sat back in his chair, laughed, and whipped his hair back. He said he would never have anything to do with that. I told him we knew about a conversation between him, his friend, and his girlfriend on the night of July 18 at the Super 8 motel. Middlekauff then conceded that there were plans for a porn site but that his only involvement with it would be to help set it up. He added that Brenda had never even met this other woman. I used this as an opportunity to add that we knew he had planned to return to La Pine, pick up Brenda, and then come back to the motel for a meeting with Brenda and this other woman to solidify their business venture.

Middlekauff then wanted to discuss the dates and times as if my accusation that Brenda had died on the night of the eighteenth was wrong. He denied that the last activity on Brenda's phone occurred on this night, saying that phone records would show her cell phone was used on the following day. I pointed out that we had all the phone records and that the last calls were to his friend (someone he had introduced to Brenda to help cover his tracks when he was with the other woman) and to his own cell phone on that night.

I offered the theory that when he had returned home and approached Brenda about the business venture, she became violent. He had to protect himself and accidently caused Brenda's death. Middlekauff sat quietly for about five seconds before saying that he loved Brenda and would never lay a hand on her. I explained that we had information about a confrontation at their home in front of the shop, where he kept his Harley Davidson, in which Brenda demanded the keys to the PT Cruiser. Middlekauff loudly asked, "When?" The other detective said it was right after Brenda's mouth surgery. (We got this information from a friend, who was told by Brenda that he had shoved her to the ground during this confrontation.) Middlekauff then acknowledged there was one incident when Brenda got information from her friend about his seeing the other woman. He said that Brenda was just frustrated. He said he was with the other woman when Brenda called and told him she had moved the Harley. He went home and found that the keypad to the shop had been disabled. The other detective and I confronted him with the information that he had knocked Brenda to the ground, and he said he didn't do anything because the remote to open the shop worked, and he found the bike still there. He added that he left Brenda standing in the drive and went back to the other woman.

We talked about the statement he had given that his friend knew nothing about what happened to Brenda. He confirmed that this statement was correct, and I explained that it would be hard for anyone to know this for sure unless they were responsible for Brenda's death and they made sure not to say anything about the murder to that friend. Middlekauff said that he understood why I believed he was responsible and added that his criminal past didn't help him. He then wanted to talk about his previous crimes and explained that while he was in California, meth did get "into the canyon of my mind." He then mentioned both kidnapping victims by name, saying that it was messed up what he had done to the first victim. He followed that up by saying he "did a carbon copy" to another woman just after getting out of prison. Middlekauff admitted that he had sexually assaulted the women but made it clear that these sex crimes had never been part of his plea bargain and therefore could never be used against him. (I honestly believe that he just didn't want to land in prison on charges relating to a sex crime and that was why he was so quick to plead guilty to the other offenses.)

Throughout the interview I looked for opportunities to push Middlekauff's buttons, as it appeared no one had ever challenged his authority or had refused to listen to his rants, and if we were unable to gain his cooperation, then I wanted to make him uncomfortable. I know I was glad the other detective was sitting in between the two of us because Middlekauff could have reached a point where he wanted to come at me. I told Middlekauff again that I knew he had killed Brenda and that we were going to prove it. He said that we would not find her body buried in his backyard and he didn't have her blood on his hands. He then walked out of the unlocked interview room.

During Middlekauff's time in the Deschutes County jail before being transferred to the custody of the state, two inmates came forward separately to talk about a poem Middlekauff had written about killers called "Crystal Teardrops." The poem, as related by the inmates, went like this: "John Wayne Gacy, he's too racy/ the Boston Strangler, he's a mangler/ Just like Ward Weaver, the cops are too dumb/ killed a woman and buried her under the house." One of the inmates said that he found it odd that the entire poem rhymed with the exception of the last lines.

The Middlekauff case remained active, and detectives followed up every lead. We also continued the tedious due diligence, but no hot leads developed during my remaining time as investigations supervisor.

My next involvement in the case came in the middle of 2005. I was on vacation when I received a phone call from a detective asking if I recalled the drive we had taken out to federal forestland approximately one mile from Middlekauff's home. I said I did, and he then asked if I recalled stopping at the small dirt speed bump just prior to going onto the federal lands, and I again said I did. He said that they had just found a body buried in a steel drum within fifty feet of where we had stopped. I knew it had to be Brenda, and I thought how odd it was that, just as in the Novakowski case, I had been so close to the victim's remains. The detectives later described that the female body was naked, bound, and gagged and had three bullet holes in the back of the head. The body was also covered in bedding identified as coming from the Middlekauff home.

I returned from vacation and, although it wasn't part of my official duties, was asked to participate in a briefing on the Middlekauff case. During the briefing, I was asked to go along with another detective to the Snake River Correctional Facility to meet with Middlekauff, explain we had found his wife, and see if he would talk.

On July 5, 2005, I was in the passenger's seat reviewing the reports when it hit me. Middlekauff had been telling us all along where Brenda was. "John Wayne Gacy, he's too racy/ the Boston Strangler, he's a mangler/ Just like Ward Weaver, the cops are too dumb/ killed a woman and buried her *in a drum*." I pulled out a picture of the partially unearthed drum and placed it in my notebook. The drive also gave me time to think back to my first interview with Middlekauff, and I realized that when I had provided him with the opportunity to say he had only defended himself against Brenda's attack, there would have been no way Middlekauff would have accepted it because he knew she was naked and bound and had been executed and then stuffed inside a metal drum. Now it was easy to understand why he had been so hesitant to admit any wrongdoing.

At the prison, the other detective and I were led into a small conference room, and at ten in the morning, Middlekauff was brought in. He made no effort to hide his dislike for me, and the other detective tried to shift his focus by reaching out his hand toward Middlekauff. Middlekauff refused to shake his hand and said simply, "I don't have anything to say to you."

I decided not to waste any more time and just explained I had the duty to inform him that we had found Brenda. Middlekauff paused, looked to his left, swallowed hard, and then weakly said "Where is she?" I said she was right where he left her. He again paused, this time pushing his hair back with his hands. Then he leaned forward and said, "Stop fucking with me." I told him that he had made it clear he didn't want to talk to us, so I didn't want him to say anything. I then reminded him of our prior conversation and my comment that I knew he had killed Brenda and that we would prove it. I then said that I thought it interesting he had been telling us all along where she was; I thought "Crystal Teardrops" was great. He stopped me. "What the fuck are you talking about?" I repeated, "Crystal Teardrops," and then recited the last lines, "Just like Ward Weaver, the cops are too dumb/ killed a woman and buried her in a drum." I tossed the photo of the partially unearthed drum onto the desk in front of him. Middlekauff then surprised me by saying that he had written "Crystal Teardrops" years ago and that it had nothing to do with Brenda. I stopped him, reminding him that he had chosen not to say anything to us. Middlekauff showed none of the emotions you would expect from someone who had just learned his wife was dead. The only emotion that was visible was his anger toward me. At 10:06 a.m., Middlekauff walked out.

Just after he left the room, the other detective and I discussed the possibility of searching his cell for any additional poems or evidence. We followed the inspector to Middlekauff's cell and stood out of sight while the inspector explained the search. At this point I heard Middlekauff talking quietly to the inspector. I thought that he had composed himself and now would start acting like a grieving husband. He was taken from the cell, and I asked the inspector what he had said. Middlekauff, thinking only of himself, said that he was afraid of the EK (European Kindred, a prison gang) and did not want to be put in general population.

We found nothing important in his cell, so we returned to Deschutes County in hopes that Middlekauff would reach out and tell someone what had taken place. We hadn't released any information about the remains, and we were careful not to share the recovery location or the cause of death. Before long we got word that he had called an acquaintance in the La Pine area close to the find and asked about a body being found, but the acquaintance wasn't aware of it.

Next we learned that another inmate had given the prison inspector a letter that Middlekauff was trying to have him send out. We obtained a search warrant for this letter, written to a girlfriend of Middlekauff's. We could only assume that he believed she had been sharing information with us, because in this letter he threatened to tell the police that she had also been responsible for putting one of the bullets into Brenda's head.

Middlekauff was set to be released from prison only to learn that Deschutes County had a warrant for his arrest. He returned to Deschutes County, and the games of hiring and firing attorneys and court challenges began. It wasn't until February 2011 that the case would go to trial. The death penalty was off the table, and the trial was set to go before a judge without a jury.

The medical examiner's testimony confirmed the identity as Brenda and the cause of death as a gunshot wound to the head. The healing of Brenda's wisdom teeth indicated that she could not have been alive at the end of July, when Middlekauff had said he had last seen her. Instead, the healing was consistent with an estimate of July 18 through 20 as the time of death.

I was called in to testify about my first interview and my contact with Middlekauff after the remains were found. Then, near the conclusion of the trial, I was called back as a rebuttal witness for the defense. The defense wanted me to say on the stand that either I had told Middlekauff or Middlekauff had overheard me talking with the other detective in the conference room about the specifics of the case, particularly how the body was found and the cause of death being bullets to the back of the head. I could only reiterate that we did not talk about those details and that the only thing I shared with Middlekauff was the picture of the partially unearthed drum.

On April 7, 2011, Middlekauff was found guilty of two counts of aggravated murder, attempted sex abuse, six counts of delivering drugs to a minor, and seven counts of sex abuse with underage girls. On Wednesday, June 1, Middlekauff was sentence to life without parole and an additional twenty-four years for the drug and sex crimes.

Chapter Fourteen

Frozen Crime Scene

At three thirty in the afternoon on October 28, 2002, the La Pine fire department responded to a fire at a Dyke Road home reported by neighbors. The house was engulfed in flames, and by the time the fire department located the body of sixty-year-old Leonard Gray, it was dark and the structure was a hazard. The decision was made to secure the home and wait until morning to remove the body.

Investigations received the call, but the victim was found near an electrical panel, so rescue personal believed the death to be accidental. The following morning the body was removed and the security was also pulled from the home. On October 30, the body of Leonard Gray was taken to the state medical examiner's office, and the examination found injuries to the skull that made his death a homicide. I received the phone call from the detective attending the autopsy, and because of the time lapse and potential loss of evidence, we scrambled to activate this investigation and resecure the crime scene.

We assigned deputies as scene security, gathered resources through the multiagency major crimes team, and set the majority of the investigation to begin the morning of October 31. That night we had a major freeze, and upon our arrival at the scene in the morning, we learned that the water that had been used to put out the fire had created a frozen crime scene, so the only area we could search was the house's exterior.

Adjacent to the scene was a vacant property, and the investigator believed we needed to sweep it for foot prints and discarded evidence. Back in the office, we found records identifying the owner of the adjacent land as a person who lived in Eugene. We tried calling this person, and we had local police in Eugene attempt contact with the owner to get permission to search; however, we were unsuccessful. At this point I decided that we had made a reasonable effort to locate the owner but had not been able to get consent, so by case law, we could search the property, as it was an open field without a fence or a "no trespassing" sign. I asked search-and-rescue volunteers to assist, and they were all lined up and ready to begin the sweep when the deputy district attorney, now on the scene, told them to stop and insisted that no search of the field could be conducted without a warrant.

I learned that I was not in charge of the scene, and my team had to shift resources to obtain a warrant before continuing. We rented propane heaters, turned them on, and let them sit in the house overnight in an effort to thaw out our crime scene. However, the next day, we found that the heat was escaping from the openings created by the fire and not thawing out the scene. Another day passed, and that weekend, I found myself and the captain covering the house with hay tarps and installing even more rented heaters in an effort to thaw the scene.

We once again rallied the major crimes team and planned on pushing the investigation forward the following morning. When we arrived at the scene early that morning, we learned that a major wind storm had knocked down a large pine tree, which was precariously resting on the fire-damaged roof.

Another day passed, and after the tree had been carefully removed, we began to process our scene. We found two dead dogs and a dead bird. As you can imagine, hopes of finding fingerprints, footprints, or blood evidence had diminished with the fire, water, and then ice, so we tried to identify what wasn't in the home to solve this case. Our thoughts were that theft or robbery could have been the motive, so we needed to find out what valuables were missing.

During one of our briefings, an investigator noted that the depth and width of the injuries to the skull were missing from the medical examiner's report. The captain rightfully believed that we needed this crucial information to identify a murder weapon. We sent detectives back to the funeral home, and I got a phone call from detectives. I then realized that if anything could go wrong with this case, it would go wrong. The detectives told me that the skull cap was now missing from the body. I said, "Of course it's missing!" I laughed, and hard. I know my reaction was unprofessional, but anyone who knows how stressful a major investigation can be also knows the sense of utter helplessness that comes at such a time, which can lead to a response such as mine that shocked the detective on the phone and humored those around me.

As we would in any homicide investigation, we needed to focus on people who may have motive, and this began with finding out about our victim. Leonard Gray was a Vietnam War vet, had his own masonry business, and was active in civic groups and had served on the Bend city council in the early '80s. In 1985, he was accused of sexually abusing two girls, ages ten and twelve, and would later plead guilty and serve time in the state prison for his crimes.

Gray went through two marriages and married a third time in 2000. His criminal record also opened the motive door for several people: the victims, their family members, or even friends who had seen what the abuse had done to them could all have been angry enough to want him dead. We also focused on Gray's business but found that most people believed he ran an honest business and worked hard for his income. However, the name of Tim Hill did come up, as he had worked for Gray for a time but ultimately had been let go.

I anxiously awaited to hear from each investigator as they completed their interview, but each time, we were left with nothing that indicated the interviewee had been involved in the crime. Tim Hill cooperated in an interview, and although the detective believed some of his behavior was unusual, he didn't find any indication that Hill had been involved in a murder and arson.

There was a report from a patrol deputy that indicated he had given Tim Hill a ride home during the early morning hours of October 28. This report also indicated that he had been walking away from the Gray residence. The deputy further stated that after he dropped Hill off, he believed he saw Hill on the road again heading toward Gray's just prior to six in the morning, when the deputy was going off duty.

The investigation continued with no solid leads. Mrs. Gray was diligent about providing descriptions of missing jewelry, and she also listed swords as missing. Here was our first piece of luck in this entire investigation: Mrs. Gray had previously allowed a family member to look at the swords to determine their value. We contacted this family member, who not only provided a detailed description of the swords but also provided his own diagrams showing every flaw, knick, and scratch.

Investigators mad up flyers with the descriptions and a photograph of the swords, and on the day they were being handed out, a detective called me and said, "I found it." Unbelievably, one of the swords had been pawned and was soon in our possession along with the pawn slip, giving us our first real lead. Optimism quickly turned to an anxious desire for justice as we learned that the individual who pawned the item lived on the streets and would not be easy to locate. We shared information with all local agencies, and it seemed like an eternity before we finally received a call that the transient had been located.

An interview team spent several hours talking with the man who had pawned the sword. Blocked by his unwillingness to be labeled a snitch and his disbelief that we were investigating a homicide, interviewers found it hard to get any information from him. Finally, the light came on that we truly were investigating a homicide. Another name new to the investigation came out of the interview, giving us another trail to follow. The game of hurry up and wait began again as we tried to track down this person, yet another transient. In the meantime we conducted searches using the names of our two transients and located a pawn store in Redmond with jewelry pawned by our second transient. We followed up by showing some of the pawned items to Mrs. Gray, who identified the jewelry as hers.

Weeks passed but finally our patrol deputies located the second transient. Detectives again were faced with convincing the subject that the items he had pawned were related to a homicide. Late in the evening, he finally provided the name of Tim Hill as the person who had provided him with the jewelry. The team put pressure on him, and he was convinced his only way out was to wear a body wire in a meeting with Hill. We arranged a motel room, took out the phone, and set a guard on the room. That night was spent writing a warrant to authorize a body wire and a subsequent search warrant for Tim Hill's residence.

As morning came, we developed a plan to have our informant stop by Hill's home and start a conversation about the pawned items and heat from the cops. We hoped that this would lead Hill to make admissions. The major crimes team was back in action. We had teams conducting surveillance and teams waiting for search warrants. We met at a local fire station to wait for approval from the deputy district attorney. Once the DA gave the blessing, we wired the informant and sent him out.

The meeting appeared natural, and Tim Hill invited our informant inside the small travel trailer that was situated on the property behind his parents' house. Unfortunately, this case had one more obstacle. As soon as the two entered the trailer the transmission from the body wire became broken and hard to decipher. The drug team commander informed me that the aluminum shell of the trailer was interfering with the radio transmission. Everyone sat in place and waited until the informant came out, and then we transported him back to the fire station for a debriefing.

The informant was animated and almost in disbelief at how casually Hill had spoken about killing Gray, the dogs, and the bird and then setting the house on fire. The informant said he wanted nothing else to do with Hill or us. He reminded us that he had kept his word and now wanted to leave. The DA was not satisfied with the debriefing and wanted us to conduct a second recorded meeting. The drug team commander agreed that we should send our informant back in, but this time with a tape recorder along with the wire. Surprised that the captain didn't immediately agree with the DA and even more surprised when he asked me what I thought our next step should be, I reminded him that we had the warrant and everyone in place to move forward. I believed that a good interview would result in admissions, and I also believed we would locate additional evidence of the crime during the search.

We moved forward with the search and arrest. I was wrong about any admissions, as Hill said nothing. The search, however, revealed an additional pawn slip issued to Hill for jewelry that was also identified as coming from the Gray home.

The following September, Timothy James Hill, who was then thirty-nine years old, pleaded guilty to murder, arson, robbery, and animal abuse and was given a life sentence. He admitted to killing Gray; stealing more than fifty thousand dollars worth of jewelry, swords, and coins; and killing two dogs and a bird in the fire, but he would not speak about the motive behind his rampage. We could only speculate. It may have been a robbery, or he may have gone to the house in an effort to get his job back, and when Gray refused to rehire him, he killed Gray and took what he wanted.

Chapter Fifteen

End of a Career

By December of 2002, I was starting to feel the effects of the stress of being on call 24-7 and holding responsibility for the recent Gray homicide, Middlekauff disappearance, and the inherited Nordstrom and Larsen missing-persons cases. I didn't think the workload could get much heavier when in came a patrol lieutenant telling me of a massive animal hoarding and abuse case. He asked for assistance, and I reluctantly offered one detective, whom the lieutenant accepted, and the lieutenant also offered to remain as the lead for the case.

The detective gathered the information and put together a search warrant for a Millican ranch, and Deschutes County soon became responsible for 129 severely neglected horses, many of which were pregnant. There are not many places where 129 horses can be kept, cared for, and monitored so their progress could be documented as evidence in a criminal case. The lieutenant did a great job of compiling resources and caring for the animals at the county fairgrounds. Lots of volunteer time, donations, and hard work went into this project, and ultimately the horses were auctioned off. The couple living on the ranch, Wayne Nichols, sixty-eight, and Rebecca Nichols, sixty-two, were each convicted of over sixty counts of animal neglect. Judge Michael Adler admittedly gave them a light sentence but acknowledged that it amounted to three days in jail for each horse that was neglected while under their care.

·   ·   ·

Early in 2003, I was assigned as the A team sergeant. This meant a return to four twelve-hour shifts, but it also meant four days off and very little chance of middle-of-the-night phone calls.

In August 2003 I was assigned as supervisor of a security team to protect President George Bush during his visit to Central Oregon to talk about the Healthy Forest Initiative. I worked the night shift out in Sunriver, where President Bush spent the night and where he also enjoyed a round of golf. I sat in a neighbor's garage, which was large enough for an indoor basketball court, and was offered smoked salmon for dinner. I didn't accept it because I knew if my troops heard that I was sitting in comfort and eating salmon during my shift while they were out around the perimeter of Sunriver, I would never hear the end of it. I got two glimpses of President Bush and was amazed at the number of well trained, and heavily armed, agents around him.

One lesson came out of this detail, at the expense of a marine deputy assigned to patrol the Deschutes River. He had approached another deputy and talked about the level of the presidential security, asking the other deputy if he had seen their scuba team in the river. The deputy said he had not seen the team and didn't think much about it. However, when the deputy commented on the scuba team in a chat with a Secret Service member, the Secret Service panicked because no such team was deployed. The information was quickly tracked back to the marine deputy, who admitted he had just been joking with the fellow deputy. Although one of our core values is a sense of humor, we also had to remember that humor is to be used only when appropriate, and as we all learned, joking about the president's security is not a laughing matter.

. . .

I checked in for my day shift, and the off-going sergeant told me that that the previous shift had investigated a fatal traffic accident on Shevlin Park Road. The car had driven off a small cliff, slammed into a large pine tree, and burst into flames. The sergeant had obtained the vehicle's information, but because of the condition of the deceased, he asked that I try to track down leads to identify who the driver was and then notify the next of kin.

My first stop was the address of the registered owner of the vehicle, and interestingly, I saw two empty gas cans sitting in front of the garage. I was unable to get anyone to answer the door, so I asked dispatch to see if they could provide any names associated with the address. They soon found the name of a woman that had previously listed that address as hers but now resided just a few houses away. I went to that house and, sadly, this was the daughter of the registered owner. She explained that her father had been suffering from a fatal disease and had lost his will to continue his fight. She had a key and allowed me into his house.

On the kitchen counter was an empty gun holster, an empty bottle of prescription drugs, a partially empty bottle of nail-polish remover, and an empty bottle of whiskey. There was a note on the counter and a cell phone with an alarm going off. I looked at the phone and saw the message, "You are nothing but a coward if you if haven't done it by now." I then read the note, from the woman's father. He explained that he loved the family but just couldn't fight the disease any longer. He said that he couldn't die a slow death, so he had drank the nail-polish remover and alcohol and taken the pills. He was then going to cover himself and his car in gas and drive off a cliff. He said just before driving off the cliff, he would set himself on fire, and as he was heading off the road, he would stick his head out the sunroof and shoot himself with his handgun.

The investigation concluded that he had been shot in the head, and the melted handgun was found inside the burned wreckage. I know that his death was devastating to his family and friends, but in police circles, we admired his commitment to getting the job done. We also agreed that no one would believe us if we shared this information.

.   .   .

The next few years went by quickly, and in August of 2007, I was promoted to lieutenant and assigned to the administrative division. One of the projects I took on was the development of a large animal rescue. I met with county administrators and animal-rescue mangers, and we developed a plan to utilize county-owned land and inmate labor to create a livestock rescue.

.   .   .

In 2008 I was again assigned as part of the security team for a visiting president. This time former President Bill Clinton came to Bend to speak on behalf of his wife, Hillary Clinton, who was running for president. I covered a back entrance to Bend High School and stood outside with several hundred people, who could not go inside because of overcrowding, waiting for a glimpse of President Clinton. After his speech, President Clinton came out the exit, saw the crowds, and then spent about twenty minutes signing autographs.

.   .   .

In August of 2010, I retired after thirty years of law enforcement service. I saw the plan for the livestock rescue come to fruition, and in February of 2011, Deschutes County received recognition as being a top defender of animal rights from the Animal Defense Fund. This national award recognized Deschutes County as setting the gold standard for protecting animals by creating one of the first known livestock rescues created and run by a sheriff's office.

When I look back at my career, I realize that stress was always present. For years I responded like the typical cop, not showing emotion, telling myself that there are some things you just don't talk about, and believing I had to accept it or get a different job. When I disagreed with a superior in the military, I would be a pain in the ass for that supervisor, causing even more frustration and stress for myself. Just like my father, I had felt the need to buy a scanner and bring my work home so that each time a call went out I got another shot of adrenalin. While in the military and at Boardman, my personal associates were also police, and this allowed me the opportunity to relive the job through the telling of war stories. I was placed into dozens of situations where I saw devastation that people are not built for prolonged exposure to. My schedule compounded the stress by requiring that I be on call twenty-four hours a day and seven days a week, and the only break came when I took vacations away from home. Then there was the shift work and the constant adjustments to my schedule to make court times, training sessions, and call-outs. Not that my career was constantly filled with fights or hair-raising events, but for each of those I encountered, I relived them in my thoughts and dreams, sometimes for years. So often I just accepted the nightmares as normal. At least weekly, I had a dream in which, during a gunfight, my handgun became inoperative. If the job wasn't bad enough already, I added even more stress while I slept.

What I have learned is that poor sleep, constant job stress, and the inability to have quality recovery time are factors that in combination are just as deadly as an armed assailant. The only difference is that we know when death is caused by the assailant, but we don't know how much life has been stolen by the silent killer.

My survival, at least up to now, could be partly attributed to the fact that I did realize early on that I needed to pursue hobbies, maintain a strong family bond, and open up with my spouse. I have also tried to remain fit through formal and informal physical activities. All I can do is hope that I will live well beyond sixty-six years of age.

My last official duty was returning to testify in the trial of Darrell Middlekauff. With his guilty verdict, I walked away feeling like the young boy placing the starfish back in the ocean. At least I have the satisfaction of knowing I helped those that I could.